Anonymous

The Present State of the British Interest in India

With a Plan for Establishing a Regular System of Government in that Country

Anonymous

The Present State of the British Interest in India
With a Plan for Establishing a Regular System of Government in that Country

ISBN/EAN: 9783337225483

Printed in Europe, USA, Canada, Australia, Japan

Cover: Foto ©Suzi / pixelio.de

More available books at **www.hansebooks.com**

THE
PRESENT STATE
OF THE
BRITISH INTEREST
IN
INDIA:
WITH A
PLAN FOR ESTABLISHING
A
REGULAR SYSTEM OF GOVERNMENT
IN THAT
COUNTRY.

LONDON:
Printed for J. ALMON, oppofite Burlington Houfe,
in Piccadilly.

MDCCLXXIII.
[Price Three Shillings.]

C O N T E N T S.

THE

PRESENT STATE

OF THE

BRITISH INTEREST

IN

INDIA, &c.

NO nation nor ftate ever acquired an acceffion of dominion fo truly valuable and beneficial, as are the acquifitions lately made by Britain in India. But the particular fituation of her circumftances at the time when thefe acquifitions fell into her hands, enhanced the real and intrinfic value of them to Britain. Oppreffed by a grievous debt, the annual intereft of which, exceeding four millions and a half fterling, was levied by taxes, which raifed the price of each manufacture, her commerce labouring under fuch difadvantages was daily finking into decay; whilft a confiderable part of this annual intereft being paid to foreigners, created fuch a drain of fpecie, as the balance of her trade could not fupply; fo that, in proportion as her expence increafed, the means of defraying it diminifhed; and fhe was eve-

B ry

ry year approaching towards a ftate of national poverty and bankruptcy.

In fuch circumftances did Britain acquire the fovereign dominion of Bengal, and of other rich manufacturing and trading countries in India ; which, at the time they fell to her, were capable of not only defraying every charge of their own government and defence, but over and above that, of yielding annually to the fovereign a fum equal to 1,300,000 l. fterling, as can be readily demonftrated. Nor do we include in this fum the benefit which Britain had been accuftomed to receive, in her commercial capacity, by her trade with thofe countries : the fum here fpecified would have arifen purely in confequence of dominion : and, whether tranfmitted from thofe countries in merchandize or in money, would at laft have arrived at the public treafury in fpecie : and would thus have ferved to alleviate the burden of thofe taxes, that are preffing every branch of her domeftic commerce to ruin. And, if Britain had beftowed the fmalleft attention on the political government of thofe countries, fhe might have continued to draw from them the above-

abovementioned tribute fum *in perpetuum,*
without any danger of draining or impo-
verifhing them: nay it is certain, that
under a juft, equitable and well ordered
government, their commerce and agriculture might have been extended to a degree, that would have enabled them to
afford a ftill larger annual tribute to the
fovereign. The poffeffion of this Indian
dominion is likewife fo particularly fecured from domeftic and foreign danger, by
the extraordinary fubmiffive difpofition of
the natives, the fingularly defenfible fituation of the country, and the naval fuperiority of Britain, that, by a very trifling
expence of men, and no pecuniary charge,
fhe might have maintained it againft all
enemies. So that Britain might have derived from this dependent dominion refources fufficient to relieve her from all
her difficulties and diftreffes.

This is what Britain might have done:
and this was not fimply poffible, it was
eafy of execution. But if we enquire
what Britain hath done, we fhall find that,
inftead of applying thefe refources by a
proper care and attention to the purpofe,
for which it would feem the all-wife dif-

penfation

penfation of Providence had at this critical conjuncture beftowed them upon her,
fhe hath indolently and defperately thrown
them from her, and left them to the will of
blind chance. For furely it may with propriety be faid, that the government of Britain configned all thefe refources to the
guidance of blind chance, or rather to
certain deftruction, when it fcrupuloufly
withheld its own care, and implicitly confided the fovereign charge of governing
and defending this foreign dominion to a
Company of Merchants, fo evidently unequal to fuch a charge, that, inftead of
being furprized that thefe countries fhould
now at laft be impoverifhed and ruined,
we have reafon to be aftonifhed, that they
have fupported, for fuch a length of time,
the complicated evils of tyranny and a-
narchy.

The confequences of committing this
fovereign charge to the Company have
been long forefeen, and likewife foretold,
by fome who were acquainted with the
nature of their government : but the
power and influence of thofe who were
fharing amongft them the plunder of thofe
wretched countries, blafted the credit of
their

their reprefentations : until at laft, the
effects being felt at home, it hath become
impoffible to totally fupprefs the truth.
Nay even now, that thefe men are forced
to partly acknowledge the ruinous fituation of this foreign dominion, yet have
they ftill the affurance to miflead the public judgment, by reprefenting the Company as the only party concerned in the
confequence : though it is certain, that
this Indian concern, which hath been
leafed or farmed out by Government to the
Company, is of the very higheft importance to the public intereft ; as having
been for many years the principal fupport
of national opulence and credit, as well
as of commerce and revenue. For, in the
article of opulence, the private fortunes
acquired in thofe countries by the fervants
of the Company, ever fince the time that
their power prevailed over the native government, that is ever fince 1757, hath
created an annual influx of fpecie to Britain of about 700,000 l. and the dedomagement paid to Government by the
Company, fince the affumption of the dewanny in 1765, is a farther influx of
400,000 l.

400,000 l. the drawback on teas is reckoned about 200,000 l. and the Company hath increased her dividend since the last mentioned period 200,000 l. though only one half of this last sum may be reckoned to remain in the country, the other half being paid to foreign proprietors. These four sums, making together 1,400,000 l. have been yearly drawn from India in consequence of dominion : and, whether sent from thence in merchandize, in bills, or in specie, have produced so much money to Britain : and notwithstanding the private fortunes have been acquired by means that have exhausted these sources of wealth, that might otherwise have flowed perpetually into Britain ; and the dedomagement may be considered as a base composition, received for alienating the sovereign rights of the British crown and nation, and for furnishing a force to support the most detestable tyranny of a few individuals over fifteen millions of men, who are to all intents and purposes British subjects ; yet did the opportune importation of so much wealth, serve to support the credit of the nation under the grievous accumulation of debt contracted in the last

war ;

war; and to prevent her feeling the drain
of fpecie made by her foreign creditors,
which otherwife would by this time have
completely exhaufted her. By her commerce with thofe countries, Britain hath
exported yearly 5 or 600,000 l. worth of
her own manufactures and merchandize,
and for thefe fhe received the commodities of India ; which commodities, being
re-exported, formed the moft effential article of her traffic with Africa, on which
her Weft India colonies do entirely depend; they are likewife the moft valuable article of her trade with America.
And the duties levied by Government, on
fuch part of thefe Indian commodities as
is expended at home, create a very confiderable, and by far the moft equitable and
convenient branch of revenue.

But the value and importance of this
Indian concern will appear in a ftill
ftronger light, if we fhall look forward to
the confequences that muft naturally and
unavoidably enfue to the public intereft
from the lofs of it. The firft and moft
immediate of thefe confequences will be
national bankruptcy; or, which is the
fame thing, a ftop to the payment of intereft

tereſt on the national debt ; for a deprivation of that annual influx of ſpecie from
India will quickly produce national poverty; and an incapacity of paying in
ſpecie the intereſt of the foreign creditors. But the loſs of our Indian commerce will operate this effect ſtill more
ſpeedily; for, on the ſuppoſition that the
nation ſhall be deprived of this branch of
commerce, it muſt neceſſarily follow, that
Government will loſe that branch of revenue which ariſes from the home conſump-
tion of Indian commodities; and it is
plain, that Government cannot then continue to pay the uſual expence, without
making good this deficiency of revenue
by additional taxes on land, and the neceſſaries of life : but as this additional
load, falling on our little remaining commerce, would by one year's experience be
found inſupportable, Government would
be forced to retrench its expence, in that
only article that can be diſpenſed with,
the payment of intereſt on the national
debt; and when this happens, what advantage will the public creditor hold above
the India proprietor ? The only difference
will be, that the latter will have felt his

loſs

lofs a little earlier than the former. But
national bankruptcy, though it may be the
firft, is not the only, nor even the great-
eft, public damage, accruing from a deprivation of this Indian concern : lofs of
future credit, of trade and navigation, and
confequently of naval power and defence,
will foon follow ; and, in this general ca-
lamity, every one individual of the community will come in for his fhare, in proportion to his rank or fituation.

Such are the confequences that muft
enfue to the public intereft from a deprivation of the benefit hitherto derived from
this Indian concern : and if the nation is
to fuffer fo grievoufly by the lofs of this
object, can fhe allow herfelf to be perfua-
ded, that fhe hath no intereft in its preferva-
tion. Now this object ftands in danger of
being loft to the nation by two different
caufes ; the firft being, the neglect or incapacity of the Company to maintain and
defend it from the affault of enemies : and
the other danger arifes from the oppreffion
and mifconduct of this Company's political government ; tending to defpoil thofe
countries of their circulating fpecie, their
arts, manufactures, commerce, and inha-

C   bitants,

bitants, which were the only means that
enabled them to afford this benefit to Britain. The firſt of theſe dangers is ſcarce-
ly dreamt of, and yet it is perhaps immediately imminent; at preſent however we
are treating of the danger to be apprehended from the political cauſe.

How far the intereſt of this foreign dominion hath been injured by the Company's political miſgovernment; or how
near it may be reduced to a ſtate of utter
inability to afford any farther benefit to
Britain, is but little known by the public.
For though people have heard in the groſs,
that affairs in thoſe countries are rather
in a bad ſituation, yet do not they either
underſtand or believe it to be ſo very bad
as it really is; or rather they do not com-
prehend how it ſhould be ſo bad; as not
being acquainted with the full power of
the cauſe that hath produced the evil;
and every one will form his notion of effects that he neither feels nor ſees, from
his knowledge or opinion of the nature and
power of the cauſes that produced them.
In the caſe before us, people have been
taught to conſider the oppreſſion and extortion of its government, (of which certain

tain inftances are quoted) as the fole caufe
of evil to Bengal: of confequence it is
fuppofed that Bengal hath fuffered no farther damage from its government, than
what may have been caufed by fome private acts of extortion, exercifed by the
few perfons vefted with the powers of
governing : and, befides that the authenticity of thefe acts is denied or difputed,
and men who are to judge only from re-
port are apt to make allowance for the
prejudice or paffion of the accufer who
brings a charge againft individuals; ftill
if all thefe acts of oppreffion that have
been narrated fhould be fully credited;
nay, if the hearer fhould fuppofe ftill
more than is reprefented, yet cannot he
conceive or allow himfelf to believe that
fuch acts of extortion, exercifed by a fmall
number of individuals, could fuffice to reduce the lately rich commercial kingdom
of Bengal to fuch a deplorable ftate of
mifery, poverty, and diftrefs : the caufe
affigned will appear too trivial for the effect; and of courfe the effect, at leaft the
degree of it, will be difcredited.

But he who means to acquire a juft notion of the prefent ftate of thofe countries,

and

and the extent of damage they have fuf-
tained from their prefent Government,
muft fully inform himfelf of the true nature and condition of that Government,
and the manner of its operation on the
general intereft of the people governed;
he muft learn, not only that which it hath
done, but likewife that which it hath not
done; for the intereft of a community may
fuffer far more detriment from the non-
action, than from the oppreffion, of its
government. To the end, therefore, that
every one may be enabled to form a proper
judgment on thefe matters, we mean to
prefent a general view of the nature, and
effects, of the Company's Government in
Bengal.

The

THE
NATURE AND EFFECTS
OF THE
COMPANY's GOVERNMENT
IN
BENGAL.

THE Englifh Eaft India company is, under the title of Dewan, the real and actual fovereign of Bengal, Behar, and Orixa : a dominion equal to almoft any one ftate in Europe, in refpect of either extent and fertility of country, or numbers of ingenious and induftrious fubjects; and exceeding moft of them in the internal materials of commerce, or refources of wealth. The Company executes the government of this dominion by a deputation, confifting of a Governor and Council; who refide at Calcutta, the Company's original prefidency, or chief factory in Bengal. And the Directors, who, as poffeffing the executive authority of the Company, may be termed the fupreme fovereigns of this Indian dominion, have preferved to themfelves the fole power of immediately ordering, directing and con-

trouling

trouling the government; for this deputed government communicates its purpofes, receives its orders, and accounts
for its conduct to none but the Directors.

But it is evident, that the diftance of
fituation muft render the immediate controul of the Directors perfectly impotent,
ineffectual, and nugatory; for it would
be abfurd to fuppofe, that the government
of Bengal fhould defer the execution of
any one purpofe until it fhall have communicated with, and received the opinion
of the Lirectors, which cannot be effected
in the fpace of a whole year; confequently
the directors cannot interfere in the direction, or ordering of this government, farther than in fume few cafes of the moft
general or invariable nature : but the
execution of even thefe general orders depends upon the will and difcretion of the
deputed government; feeing the Directors
cannot, at that diftance, enforce it themfelves : and the fame caufe puts it out of
their power to prevent or reftrain abufe;
fo that they hold neither pofitive nor ne-
gative authority in the immediate execution of this government. And the condition or fituation of thefe directorial fovereigns

vereigns at home, renders their retrof-
pective controul equally impotent and ineffectual ; for they have no power in themfelves to inflict other punifhment on their
deputies, for the moft audacious difobedience, or for maladminiftration, than dif-
miffion from their fervice ; and this becomes no punifhment, becaufe the delinquents are previoufly prepared for it, being
ready to fet out of their own accord with
a princely fortune for the mother country;
where they fet the authority of the Directors at defiance ; for there thefe fovereigns of India are themfelves fubjects, and
cannot call their quondam minifters to account, except in an ordinary court of juftice ; and the difficulty of obtaining evidence requifite to convict in thefe courts;
the dread of bringing to light, in the
courfe of a legal procefs, fome abftrufe
myfteries of government; and the apprehenfion of danger arifing to the intereft
of the prefent direction from a powerful
combination at the next election, will ever
deter the Directors from ferioufly profecuting a lawfuit againft their deputies,
even in cafes of peculation from the fovereign ; but if it refpects only the intereft

of

of the fubject, they will be more apt to
palliate and defend the offence. We muft
therefore perceive, that this deputed government acts perfectly independent of
either the immediate controul, or future
awe of the fovereign: whilft the fovereign
is compelled to blindly fupport, with its
whole power, the authority of this government; and, without choice, to enforce all its meafures; feeing that to oppofe the will of the deputy, is oppofing
the authority of the fovereign.

And, as to the native fubjects, the power
of this deputed government over them is
perfectly abfolute and complete. For the
inhabitants of thofe countries, being difpofed by nature or climate to paffive obedience, and by long cuftom habituated to
defpotic authority, and being farther im-
preffed with a particular awe of Europeans,
from a notion of their natural fuperiority,
implicitly fubmit to the will of their prefent government, without once daring to
either examine its right, difpute its authority, or queftion its conduct. The
fubject therefore holds not the fmalleft
voice in the adminiftration of government; the jurifdiction, the police, the
finances,

finances, the military government and defence, are all incontroulably directed by the Company's deputation : and the entire interests of thofe countries, the lives and property of the inhabitants, are fubjected to its difcretion, and depend on its will.

So that this deputation of the Company executes the government of Bengal with a power perfectly unlimited by any exterior controul ; and if we confider that it is at the fame time foreign to the country governed, mutable, and of very fhort duration, we fhall find that it is equally unreftrained by any internal check. It is therefore the moft unlimited government on earth; or rather it is the only government that can, with propriety, be termed arbitrary and defpotic.

For all other deputed governments are fufficiently reftrained by the authority of the fovereign ; and we have no idea of defpotifm, except in governments that are fupreme or fovereign. But the idea of actual defpotifm in a fupreme government is merely imaginary ; feeing that, in one and all of thefe governments, the power of governing is conditional, limited by

D   rule,

rule, and fubjected to controul both external and internal. For it is evident,
that, in all fupreme governments, the
power of governing, and the means that
fupport this power, muft needs be derived
from the people governed; and therefore cannot exift in defpight of their confent; and though, in fome of thefe governments, the condition, upon which
this power and thefe means are granted, is
not fpecially expreffed, yet is it perfectly
underftood, and invariably enforced in all
of them; inafmuch as there are examples
in each, of fovereigns who have fuffered
the utmoft punifhment, for attempting to
tranfgrefs the limits of this condition;
nay, there is fcarce one inftance where
the prince, thus tranfgreffing, efcaped the
refentment of the people; and examples
of this nature are moft frequent in thefe
governments that are falfely termed defpotic. Thefe examples muft therefore
convince all fovereigns, that there is a
power in the people, fuperior to, and
capable of controuling them; and the
fenfe of this muft ever prove an effectual
external controul on the conduct of a fupreme government. But felf-intereft,
that

that *primum* and *perpetuum mobile* of human
action, which we may term an internal
check, operates still more forcibly, con-
stantly, and immediately on the will of a
supreme government; not simply reftraining it from doing or permitting injury, but
impelling it to promote the good of the
people governed. For a government that
is fovereign, and perpetual (or *durante
vita* and hereditary) cannot poffibly feparate its own private intereft from that of
the community which it governs; being
indeed itfelf a part of that community:
and this is fo evident, that no prince ever
attempted to advance a diftinct intereft of
his own, at the expence of the general
weal, who was not a fool, before he became
a tyrant. But a wife fovereign confiders
his people as the channel through which
alone he can receive fubftantial good or
evil; and, acting upon this principle, he
will, however abfolute and difpofed by
nature to tyranny, abftain from injuring
the general intereft, becaufe he is fenfible that fuch injury will recoil upon himfelf; and he will exert himfelf to promote the profperity of his people, as the
only means of advancing his own power,

gran-

grandeur, or wealth. So that a fovereign prince, who underftands his own real intereft, though otherwife void of virtue, will ever ftudy to govern well ; nay, the private vices of fuch a prince do often operate public good ; a ftriking inftance of which we meet with in our Henry the Seventh ; whofe extreme and fordid avarice was the fource of Englifh commerce and wealth ; and his mean felf-love, and jealoufy of power, eftablifhed univerfal liberty.

But the nature of this Bengal government differs, in every circumftance, from that of a fupreme government ; being deputed, foreign, mutable, and temporary, it is no way interefted in the lafting profperity of the community which it governs ; on the contrary, this government holds an intereft which is not only diftinct from, but diametrically oppofite to that of the fubject. For thefe Governors return to Europe immediately on the expiration of their office, which feldom dures above three years, often lefs ; therefore their fole aim is to amafs all the wealth they can, during the fhort term of their power, in order to tranfport it along with their

perfons

perfons to their own country. But the wealth which a government amaffes, muft needs be extorted from the people governed; confeqnently felf-intereft leads this government to pillage and plunder the fubject: and we have feen that it is not reftrained, by any external controul, from advancing its own diftinct intereft at the expence of the community which it governs, feeing it is perfectly exempted from all awe of either the fovereign or the fubject; and it cannot be reftrained by any internal check, becaufe it holds no concern in the lafting welfare of the people.

Such then is the ruling principle of this government : nor are the means which it employs to promote its own intereft lefs extraordinary than is its power to enforce them. For this government, which arbitrarily directs the jurifdiction and police, together with the impofition and collection of taxes, doth at fame time act in the capacity of a merchant. And this commercial defpotifm, or defpotic power lodged in the hands of a few foreign merchants, hath, in its nature and confequences, proved infinitely more deftructive to the intereft of that commercial country,

country, than all the operations of political tyranny have been : for from it fprung thefe cruel monopolies, which ftruck at the very root of manufacture, commerce, and even population.

To attempt defcribing the particular methods which this government hath prac-tifed to promote its own intereft at the expence of the people, in its double ca-pacity, of an abfolute fovereign and a def-potic merchant, would be a tedious, in-vidious, and even an unprofitable under-taking; for it is almoft impoffible to pro-perly delineate the conduct of a tyranny fo various and irregular in its operations; and, to thofe who are unacquainted with the modes, cuftoms, and interefts of the country in queftion, the recital of a few particular inftances would only ferve to miflead their judgment, and darken or di-minifh the truth. By attending to the general defcription given of the nature views and interefts of this government, we fhall form a more complete and juft notion of its conduct and deportment, than can be acquired from any disjointed ac-count of particulars. Let us fuppofe a few foreigners fent into a rich commercial country,

country, with abfolute and unlimited
power over the lives and property of the
inhabitants; actuated by no other principle
than that of acquiring riches, and ftimu-
lated thereto not only by avarice but ambition, or the defire of excelling ; unreftrained by any fpecies of prefent awe or
future apprehenfion ; but on the contrary,
encouraged by precedent to expect in their
own country, titles, dignity, refpect, and
confequence, each in proportion to the
fum he imports; and whatever methods
we can fuppofe would be practifed by fuch
foreigners, to accomplifh their purpofe,
within a fhort limited term, we may fuppofe to have been actually employed by
this Bengal government. The enormous
amount of numerous fortunes, imported
by the perfons employed in this government, together with the rapidity of acquifition, are circumftances feen and known
in this country ; and thefe will thoroughly
warrant our fuppofing, that the acquirers
have availed themfelves to the utmoft of
their powers, as well as their opportunities. However, we fhall err greatly in
our eftimate of the damage caufed to thofe
countries, by their government's profecuting

cuting its own diftinct intereft, if we fhall
confine the reckoning to only the lofs of
fo much fpecie, as hath been extorted and
exported by thefe foreigners: for this,
though in itfelf a ruinous grievance, is
merely trivial, when compared with the
havoc and wafte committed on the manufacture, the commerce, agriculture, and
population, by the methods employed to
acquire thefe fums. A herd of hogs,
broke into a well dreffed vineyard, will
gorge their voracious maws; but that
which they eat and devour doth not de-
ftroy the vineyard; it is their manner of
eating, their rutting up, their tearing
down, and trampling under foot.

Hitherto we have regarded this government in only one point of view: we have
feen it acting for itfelf; but we have not
feen the part it acts for the people, in its
capacity of a fovereign ruler, adminiftring
the government of a mighty ftate in all
its different offices or departments; and
entrufted with the care of the whole and
entire interefts of a numerous commercial
nation. But, in the difcharge of this fovereign truft, we fhall find the government of Bengal a mere *Vis inertiæ*, void
of

of the two efficient principles of action, ability or power of acting, and will or inclination. For how can we expect to find the ability, of governing well, in the men employed by the Company to execute the government of those countries? to attain the knowledge of any one science or mystery, demands an effort of the mind; but it is impossible for the brightest natural genius to arrive at even a moderate degree of skill in the art of governing, which, as it is the most elevated, so is it the most difficult, abstruse, various and complicated of all human sciences, without long and intense application, study, and reflection; and, we may add, a series of practice; and all these gradations to skill, in governing, are wanting to our Bengal governors. Their scholastic education extends no farther than to qualify them for merchants clerks; and, immediately on being taken from school, they are dispatched to India; where the manner of life is consonant to the climate, voluptuous to a degree of dissoluteness, vain, idle, dissipated, and an enemy to study or reflection: the juvenile part of their life being spent in this manner, they ar-

rive

rive at the charge of government with minds perfectly uninformed, and fo very averfe to application, that they commit and implicitly confide the charge of their own private concerns to fervants. If fuch men fhould poffefs the fkill or addrefs of governing well, it muft certainly be acquired inftantaneoufly and fupernaturally ; infufed into them by miracle, like the gift of fpeech into the afs of Balaam.

But the want of will or inclination is an obftacle to their governing well, ftill more prevalent than is the want of ability. Labour, fatigue, and difficulty are evils, to which the human mind is fo naturally averfe, that, unlefs it is urged by fome ftrong impulfe of paffion, fuch as the fear of fome fuperior evil, or the hope and defire of fome mighty good, it will decline and evade them : what ftimulum then can be fufficiently powerful to urge the habitually indolent minds of our Bengal governors to encounter the difficulties, the labour, and fatigue attending a due difcharge of the duties of government; which, of all human undertakings, is the moft replete with thefe mental evils ? Yet this government, which demands a ftron-

ger

ger ftimulum than any other government that ever yet exifted, is in effect urged by no one motive or confideration to difcharge the duties of its office ; for, as it holds no intereft in the lafting welfare of the people governed, neither its hopes nor its fears are at all interefted in the good or evil confequences that may be caufed by its own vigilance or neglect : being altogether fuperior to the refentment of the fubject, and independent of the fovereign's authority, it is not impelled, by the fear of immediate danger, nor the apprehenfion of future punifhment : and as to the profpect of glory, applaufe, or refpect, which pufh the generous and ambitious mind to action, our governors aim to attain them, not by governing well, but by acquiring and bringing home a mighty fortune to their own country.

Men thus actuated, or rather unactuated, muft, in the difcharge of their fovereign office, be perfectly torpid aud liftlefs ; the machine of political government ftops in their hands, and ftands ftock ftill : their minds being incapable of application, they withdraw themfelves as much as poffible from attention, and leave the trouble

of

of governing to others, ſtill leſs qualified
than themſelves; theſe inferior agents being
choſen, not for their abilities or virtue, but
for their fitneſs to ſerve the private purpoſe
of the governors, otherwiſe by chance; but
they give themſelves no trouble to inſpect
the conduct of theſe agents, who in general are unprincipled miſcreants; on the
contrary, they promiſcuouſly approve and
ſupport every action; ſo that, wherever
the power of this government acts, it is
only to oppreſs; and all beſide is left to
chance. However, the power of governing, or rather of oppreſſing, is not confined to the perſons veſted with the charge
of government: the numerous ſervants
whom this Company diſperſes over the
face of the country, for the purpoſe of
carrying on her trade, do each of them,
in his own diſtrict, aſſume the authority
of a deſpot; and communicates a like
authority to all his ſervants and dependants, who, it muſt be allowed, are far
more unrelenting than their maſters; and
thus tyranny is extended into every corner;
oppreſſion becomes general; and the op-
preſſed are excluded from the very proſ-
pect of redreſs; for, on appeal to the
ſuperior,

superior, the plaintiff is ever remanded to the very oppreffor, who punifhes him for having dared to complain. And thus juftice and protection are no where to be found; vice goes unpunifhed, and innocence unfupported; therefore every man becomes a villain in his own defence; and faith, confidence, truth, and honefty are banifhed the land. In fhort, it may with ftrict propriety be faid by thefe wretched peo le, *Terras aftræa reliquit*; and tyranny and anarchy have here fet up their throne.

And to this inaction or non-exertion of the powers of government we are to impute the ruin of thofe countries, rather than to the avarice or rapine of the perfons deputed by the Company to execute that government. For the power of governing being vefted in only a few, the extortion of thefe few might have been long fupported by a rich commercial country, provided they had exerted themfelves to reftrain and prevent all others from plundering and oppreffing. The avarice, profufion and bloody tyranny of even Nero, and Domitian, was felt by only a few of their fubjects at Rome; every where elfe the empire flourifhed; be-

caufe

caufe thefe imperial monopolizers of vice would fuffer none in power to be wicked but themfelves; they narrowly infpected the conduct of their governors and offi- cers, and feverely punifhed their injuftice or oppreffion. But where the govern- ment doth not only plunder itfelf, but fuffers every one under it to plunder, that country muft in time be completely ruined.

Now Bengal hath been fubjected to a government of this nature for thefe fifteen years paft; for though we commonly date the commencement of the Company's fo- vereignty from the affumption of the De- wanny, (as it is termed,) yet hath this Company (at leaft her deputies) poffeffed a really abfolute authority in thofe coun- tries ever fince the battle of Plaffey in 1757. That action rendered them maf- ters of Bengal; and it was equally within their power to affume the fovereign go- vernment at that time, as afterwards in 1765; their own will was the only ob- ftacle: but notwithftanding they beftowed it on a native Nabob, yet did they retain an abfolute fuperiority over him, and he governed in a ftate of perfect fubordina- tion

tion to their authority ; for he well knew and experienced, that the duration of his office, and even of his exiftence, depended upon their will ; confequently this dependent native government could but little reftrain the conduct of the Company's deputies, or protect the fubject from their rapacity ; and when they, in 1765, fet afide this native government, they only removed a fcreen which they themfelves had fet up, and till then preferved for their own purpofe.

How far thefe countries may have advanced towards the period of final ruin, under the fifteen or fixteen years domination of fuch a government, we fhall not pretend to determine, becaufe the term *ruin* is varioufly underftood. This much is certain, that the unbounded remittance of fpecie made, for fome years, by the Englifh Company, for fundry purpofes as fovereign ; and for a much greater number of years, and in much larger fums by the other European Companies, who received it from the fervants of the Englifh Company for bills on Europe, at a very low exchange, and employed it for every purpofe in the other parts of India

and

and China, hath compleatly drained Bengal of its wealth, and reduced it to a state of the most abject poverty. And the grievous oppression and rapine exercised by the Company's servants, and their numerous dependants; together with the most cruel monopolies usurped by them over every species of merchandize, and even the neceſſaries of life, hath in a great meaſure ſuppreſſed commerce, and abolished trade. Whilst the inſatiable avarice and unreſtrained extortion of thoſe employed in the collection of taxes and revenue having ruined the farmer, the lands lay uncultivated and waſte ; inſomuch that, not to mention the immenſe decreaſe of revenue, that naturally moſt fertile of all countries, Bengal, hath ſuffered a more ſevere famine than perhaps was ever heard of; it being reckoned that a fifth part of the inhabitants have died of want, and numbers have fled from ſtarving and oppreſſion.

But it is not difficult to determine how near the intereſt of Britain in thoſe countries hath approached to ruin : for Britain is to conſider them as ruined to her purpoſe, ſo ſoon as they ſhall become incapable of ſupporting a commerce beneficial

cial to her; and at fame time of yielding
her a confideration, in the nature of tribute, equivalent to the expence of fubjects which fhe fends out annually to maintain her dominion there. And that they
are nearly, if not totally, ruined to her,
in both thefe refpects, we begin already
to feel, in fpite of all the art or influence
ufed to conceal the truth.

For, in the article of tribute, we find
that, inftead of receiving fuch a furplus
of revenue as fufficed, at the commencement of the Dewanny, to not only pay
for the fpecie part of the Company's inveftment in Bengal itfelf, but to purchafe
her cargoes, and defray all her charges in
the other parts of India, and in China,
the government of Bengal was, two years
ago, reduced to the neceffity of borrowing near a million fterling on bills, which
have been tranfmitted and accepted by the
Company : in like manner hath this government been obliged to borrow laft year;
though the bills have been prevented, by
an arbitrary ftroke of deceit, from appear-
ing againft them in Europe. Thefe borrowed fums have all been expended in Bengal itfelf: and if we allow that the whole
F   hath

hath been employed to pay for the Company's inveftment, (though by the by the fpecie part of the Company's inveftment cannot, at leaft it ought not, if fhe exports the proper quantity of European commodities, exceed half a million,) it muft even then be admitted, that the revenue of Bengal hath barely fufficed to defray the ordinary expence of government. And, if fo, from whence is the tribute of Bengal, (whether we term it dedomagement, drawback, or encreafed dividend) to arife? not from the mighty cargoes imported; for they are purchafed, not with furplus revenue, but with borrowed money, which muft be repaid either in India or in Europe : and as to the profits on thefe cargoes, they will be more than eat up by the charges of freight, and a long reckoning of India intereft at eight per cent. I am fenfible, that this account is ftrangely perplexed and embarraffed by intricate calculations of ftock in hand, annual importations, and future fales, &c. but when divefted of all thefe ftudied intricacies it will ftand fimply thus—As is the clear furplus of revenue received in Bengal, fo will be the amount of tribute
received

received in Britain ; the former will ever exactly balance the latter. But this furplus we find to have been, for the two paft years, equal to nothing ; and the amount of tribute received in Britain muft amount to exactly as much ; confequently the dedomagement, drawback, and increafed dividend for the two laft years is ftill *in Nubibus*; where the national part, confifting of the two firft articles, is like to remain ; unlefs it fhall be paid out of the Company's capital ftock, as the encreafed dividend hath been. But this revenue, which for the two years paft hath barely fufficed to defray the expence of government, hath not been kept up even to that extent without the aid of violence : but violence itfelf muft yield to neceffity, and cannot extort that which doth not exift ; moreover the Company had, in thefe two years, decreafed her military expence, by difbanding fome thoufand fipahis, and otherwife diminifhing the charge of her remaining force ; and the attack made by Shaw Allum in conjunction with the Mharrattors will, this year, compel her to re-augment her military expence in every refpect ; whilft the predatory incurfions of thefe

Mhar-

Mharrhattors will prevent the collection of revenue; how then will she support the augmented charge of this year, with a revenue decreased by a variety of caufes so much below the degree of laft year? Another loan upon the ftrength of the capital is the only refource; but poffibly borrowing may, for several reafons, have become impracticable by this time; and it is certain that troops will not, nay cannot, ferve without pay—Here is a blefled profpect indeed.

But, leaving this to the proof of time, we perceive that, at any rate, we have loft the profpect of future tribute from Bengal, through the channel of the Company; wo have not fo much as the promife of dedomagement, drawback, or encreafed dividend for this current year; and if wo can truft to our own reafon, preferably to bankrupt promifes, we may give it up for good and all. Nay, there is mighty reafon to apprehend, that even the private fortunes will foon ceafe to exift; and then Britain will ceafe to receive the fum of 1,400,000 l. fterling, which for a number of years paft hath been annually flowing in to her from India, in confequence of domi-

dominion. And if fhe could barely fupport her burden, when aided by this influx,
how will fhe, when deprived of it, anfwer the annual drain of fpecie made by her
foreign creditors ?

With refpect to the prefent ftate of our
commerce with thofe countries, it is not
enquired, and therefore not known, whether the Company exports the ftipulated
fum of Britifh commodities or not; and it
is ftill lefs known, whether the fmall
quantity fhe hath exported of late is difpofed of; or whether it remains in her
warehoufes abroad, to fwell up the account of her ftock; thus much however
reafon tells us, that the inhabitants of
Bengal, who cannot procure the neceffaries of life, millions having died of
want, can but little afford to purchafe foreign fopperies or fuperfluities. Neverthelefs we have feen large cargoes of Indian manufactures imported this very year;
but we are not to fuppofe, that thefe cargoes are the produce of willing induftry;
they are procured by force and compul-
fion; the artifan being held to work under
the difcipline of tafk mafters, who de-
prive him of his labour before it is completed,

pleted, at a price that will not afford him the means of living. Of the many markets that for ages had taken off the manufactures of Bengal, Europe is now the only one remaining; and this one market cannot be supplied without the application of force. How long force might supply the place of willing industry, we shall not pretend to determine; but one year more will discover the united effects of want of artisans, want of money, and Mharrattor incursions.

And thus have we demonstrated the nature and condition of this Bengal government, together with the evils it hath caused to the country governed, not from a recital of disputed facts, but from principles universally understood and admitted. For every one, the least acquainted with the Company's affairs, must know and will allow that the views, the interests, the powers and opportunities of her deputed government in Bengal are exactly such as we have described them; and upon this one undisputed *datum* we have built our whole demonstration; the truth and justness of which every man is capable of trying and proving, by the touchstone of

his

his own reafon. For reafon, without the
aid of circumftantial proof, can judge
whether the line of conduct which we
have affigned to the government of Bengal, is fairly inferred and deduced from
its evident and allowed principle of action ;
and common fenfe, unaffifted by demon-
ftration, will point out the effects that
fuch conduct muft operate on the intereft
of the country governed ; and, if we farther advert to the length of time that this
country hath been fubjected to fuch operation, we fhall nearly guefs at its prefent
ftate and condition.

And we doubt not, that what hath been
faid will enable every one, who makes ufe
of his own reafon and reflection, to form a
proper judgment for himfelf on certain
points of this Eaft India bufinefs, which
have been moft grofsly mifreprefented.
For he will thereby difcover, that the object, for which the nation hath to apprehend at prefent, is not the " *credit* of
the Company ;" which, had fhe been reftrained within her natural fphere, and her
conduct properly infpected by government,
could never have been injured ; or, if it
had, the breach could (in fuch cafe) have
little

little more affected the general weal, than the failure of any large trading house; which, so long as the trade remained entire, would have been immediately replaced by another; but he will perceive, that the present bad state of the Company's credit is only an effect, or consequence, of the ruinous situation of affairs in India; and, of course, that the object of national apprehension is the ruin or loss of that mighty and important branch of national interest, which hath been committed to the charge of the Company, in a manner so complete and implicit, that the name, as well as the interest of the nation, nay the very name of the object itself, hath been sunk and lost in that of the Company: this Company, which is but the temporary farmer, having been, to all intents and purposes, substituted in the stead of not only the sovereign proprietor, but even of the farm itself. And it will farther appear, that the danger which threatens this object is not to be averted by blindly supporting the credit of the Company: but, on the contrary, that the nation will, by affording this blind support, only furnish the means of com-

completing that ruin, which is already fo far advanced. To prevent this danger demands meafures of a very different nature: and we fhall proceed to point out thefe meafures; which, had they been applied in time, would, we humbly conceive, have fufficed to prevent the ruin or lofs of this important concern: and which, if matters are not paft remedy, may yet ferve to reftore them.

G   THE

THE TRUE CAUSES OF

EVIL AND ABUSE

IN THE

GOVERNMENT OF BENGAL,

AND THE

MEANS TO REMEDY THEM.

IT is a common faying that, the caufe of an evil being known, the remedy is readily difcovered; and, upon the ftrength of this maxim, feveral, who think they have hit upon fome one caufe of evil in the political government of Bengal, have taken upon them to prefcribe a remedy; which is pronounced an univerfal panacea, a falve for every fore: but no fooner have they produced their ware, than the eye hath difcovered it to be mere powder of poft; or fomething equally unavailing.

Few of thefe prefcriptions have at all attracted notice; the propofal for protecting the liberty of the fubject from the defpotifm of government, by the inftitution of native juries, was indeed extremely well calculated to pleafe Britifh fpeculation; and therefore, like the device of hanging the bell about the cat's neck, it was

highly

highly applauded by thofe who never adverted to the difference betwixt Britain and Bengal, in point of general conftitution of government and difpofition of the natives. But, for practice, it muft appear a mere chimera to fuch as confider, on the one hand, that men, who are flaves to their government and its officers in every other capacity, cannot poffibly be free in that of jurymen ; and that juries, if they are not free and impartial, avail nothing : and, on the other hand, that if the natives fhould be actually endowed with the real cap of liberty in the jury room, there is danger, nay, there is a certainty, that they would make bold to wear it elfewhere ; and then, adieu to the Englifh dominion in Bengal. In few words, the power of the Englifh government, and the freedom of native juries, are two things that cannot poffibly exift together in Bengal; the life of the one muft unavoidably caufe the death of the other : and, however harfh this doctrine may found in a freeborn Englifh ear, the force and truth of it will immediately ftrike the politician.

Equally

Equally unavailing is that proposal for
securing the liberty and property of the
subject, from the oppreffion and extortion
of government, by granting to the native
a perpetual property in land; without pro-
viding him the fmalleft fecurity for the
free poffeffion of its produce; which, fo
long as government ftands on its prefent footing, is liable to be wrefted from
him fo foon as acquired.

But it would feem, that the reafon why
thefe political phyficians have been fo un-
lucky in their prefcriptions is, that they
have proceeded upon falfe principles; as
having miftaken the nature of the malady.
For they have either affigned no one certain
caufe of evil; or elfe they have traced it
no farther than to the perfons who have
executed the government of thofe countries, otherwife to the Directors : as if all
the evil had proceeded from fome particular vicioufnefs in their difpofition, as if
they had been finners above all men, or
as if no men would have done the wicked
deed but they : whereas he who is the
leaft acquainted with human nature will
allow, that few, if any men, would have
made any better ufe of their powers and

oppor-

opportunities; nay he will add, that every
other government on earth, would act the
very part that this Bengal government
hath done, provided it held the fame views
and interefts, together with the fame powers and opportunities. And, if fo, what
can be more abfurd, than the propofal to
remedy the evils and abufes of this go-
.vernment, by fending out Supervifors,
with the fame or greater powers, and confequently poffeffing greater opportunities
of promoting their own views and interefts; which are exactly the fame as thefe
of the perfons complained of; feeing that,
as the fame caufe of evil which exifted in
the Governors, would have exifted in the
Supervifors, thefe fimilar caufes muft have
operated fimilar effects.

Indeed we fhall err widely, if we look
for the original caufe of evil in thefe Governors: for, on infpecting the preceding
defcription of this Bengal government, we
perceive, that their maladminiftration is
itfelf but an effect, or confequence, naturally flowing from the total want of certain fundamental principles or powers;
which, in every other government, ferve
to reftrain the party governing from do-

ing

ing or permitting injury, and impel it to
promote the good of the party governed:
and as the want of thefe reftraining and
impelling powers hath unavoidably produced, the firft tyranny, and the latter
anarchy, it is plain, that all the evils and
abufes in the government of Bengal have
fprung from this deficiency. It farther
appears, from the fame defcription, that
the want of thefe reftraining and impelling powers arifes from two different
caufes; the firft being the particular condition and conftitution of the fovereign:
and the fecond is there termed the diftance of fituation, betwixt the fovereign
refidence and the country governed; tho'
the fequel will evince this latter to be rather a radical defect in the nature of that
fyftem, which the Directors have adopted
for the government of this diftant dominion. That thefe have been the two original caufes of the tyranny and anarchy,
and confequently of all the evils and a-
bufes in this Bengal government, includ-
ing thefe of the commercial defpotifm, is
fufficiently evident. We fhall therefore
proceed to point out the means of remov-
ing thefe caufes, as the only effectual method

thod of remedying the evils. And as
each of the two caufes hath contributed
its proper fhare of the evil, and each demands a diftinct remedy, we fhall confider them feparately.

With regard to the condition and conftitution of the Company, we have already
mentioned the feveral circumftances that
difqualify her for the office of a fupreme
fovereign ; here therefore we fhall only
recapitulate, or collect them into one point
of view. The firft defect is, her impotence, or want of power to promote good
government in her dominion : and this
proceeds from her being, with refpect to
her deputed government, a meer fellow
fubject, totally void of fupreme legiflative and judicial powers ; and confequently
incapable of inforcing obedience; or of
punifhing difobedience : and this want of
authority and power in the fovereign, we
have fhown to be a principal caufe of defpotifm in the deputed government. A
fecond defect in the conftitution of the
Company is her want of inclination, or
rather of intereft, to difcharge the duty
of a good fovereign ; and this arifes from
the fluctuating and hourly mutable ftate
of

of the proprietary, the temporary and
fhort duration of her corporate exiftence,
the ftill fhorter tenor of this fovereignty,
and the annual rotation of her executive
government; for, in cohfequence of thefe
feveral circumftances in her fituation, her
views are narrow, contracted, and rapacious; the fole aim of all her meafures
being to make the moft of the prefent
moment. The third defect is the mercantile capacity of this fovereign. Company; and from this defect alone flow
evils fufficient to ruin the intereft of the
country fubjected to her government:
for, in confequence of her mercantile capacity, her deputed government acts as a
merchant; and, in confequence of her
fovereign capacity, all her mercantile fervants affume the authority of fovereigns.

Thefe are the principal defects in the
being and conftitution of this fovereign
Company; and it is evident, that fuch
defects in the fovereign, muft have contributed largely towards the exiftence of
abufe, in the deputed government. But
thefe defects might have been, in a great
meafure, remedied, and their confequences prevented, by a fimple act of parliament,

ment, paſt by the national government, at the time it thought proper to commit the charge of this important branch of national intereſt, to the care of the Company. This act might have been entitled, " An act for better enabling the Eaſt India Company to adminiſter the political government, and to protect, maintain and defend certain ſtates and countries in India, which have become ſubjected to the dominion of Britain, and which, for ſundry weighty conſiderations, it hath been judged proper to commit to her charge." And it might have been conceived in the following, or ſuch like terms.

" Whereas it appears, that the want of a proper legiſlative authority over the miniſters and ſervants, employed by the Company to execute the ſovereign government of theſe ſubjected dominions, muſt be productive of many abuſes, detrimental as well to the intereſt of the Company, as to the honour and intereſt of the Britiſh nation. Be it enacted by &c. that, from the time of paſſing this act, the Company ſhall poſſeſs the power of legiſlation, or making laws, for the government of this foreign dominion: and the laws thus

H   enacted

enacted by the Company, fhall be equally
binding on all her minifters, fervants, and
fubjects, in that dominion, as are the acts
of parliament on the fubjects of Britain.
And being farther fenfible of the many
inconveniences, that muft arife from the
Company's incapacity of punifhing the
offences committed by her minifters, and
fervants abroad, otherwife than by applying to courts of juftice that are foreign
to her government; where fhe cannot
convict, through the difficulty of obtaining the evidence required by the forms of
thefe courts; and where fhe is deterred
from profecuting, by the fear of divul-
ging the fecrets of her government; infomuch that, rather than apply to thefe
courts, fhe muft fubmit to the moft audacious acts of difobedience, and maladminiftration; and confidering that fuch incapacity in the Company muft difcourage all
good government, and produce tyranny
and anarchy in this dominion; be it
enacted, that the Company fhall have authority to erect courts of juftice, and appoint judges; with the like powers, as
are vefted in his majefty's judges, and
courts of judicature, for trying and judging

ing all fuits and caufes, or offences committed within the limits of this Indian
dominion; and for punifhing the fame,
either capitally, or by fine, imprifonment,
and banifhment, though to Europe only.
And whereas it is probable, that fome of
the minifters or fervants of the Company
may, by various methods, elude the juftice of her courts abroad, and efcape to
Europe; in order therefore to prevent fuch
dangerous illufion of juftice, it is enacted,
that the Company's court of directors
fhall, on due information being made to
them, have power at all times to call before them fuch efcaping delinquents, and
to try and punifh them, for the offences
they may have committed within the limits of this Indian dominion, in like
manner as they could have been tried or
punifhed by the Company's courts abroad.
And becaufe the liberty of appealing from
the Company's courts of juftice, to the
judgment of any other courts, muft be
productive of the fame inconveniences to
the Company, as a trial of the fame caufe
in the firft inftance would have been, and
muft therefore deter the Company from
ever availing herfelf of the judicial powers

granted

granted by this act; it is enacted, that
delinquents shall have no liberty of appealing from the Company's courts abroad,
excepting to the Court of Directors at
home, or to a general court of Proprietors; whose judgment in all such cases
shall be final. And as the Court of Directors have, and may be, discouraged,
from prosecuting or punishing the crimes
of their rich servants, by the fear of danger to their own private interest, from a
combination of the friends and abettors
of such rich delinquents at a future annual
election, be it enacted, that the 24 Directors, being such at the time of passing this
act, shall continue in office, *durante vita.*"

" And whereas it appears, that the
liberty of daily selling, transferring, and
alienating the shares in the Company's
stock, of which this sovereign dominion
forms a part, tends to infuse into the proprietors a spirit of rapacity, that may be
productive of much damage to the several
interests concerned; and hath many other
very pernicious consequences; whilst it
reflects disgrace on the dignity of all other
sovereigns; be it enacted, that no proprietor in this Company's stock, of which
the

the fovereignty forms a part, fhall have power to fend his fhare in the faid fovereignty to market, like as it were a hog or bullock, and to fell, transfer, and alienate the fame; but that the feveral proprietors of this ftock and fovereignty, being fuch at the time of paffing this act, fhall remain and continue proprietors, without the power of alienation, except in the cafes that fhall be hereafter fpecified.

And whereas it hath been reprefented that the Company's holding this fovereignty by leafe, and for a fhort term, may not only alienate her care and prevent her from ftudying and promoting the lafting welfare of the country, but may induce her to pillage, plunder and wafte it; be it enacted, that the Company fhall hold the fovereignty of this dominion, *quamdiu fe bene gefferit*; to the end, that fhe may confider and treat it, not as the property of another, but as her own inheritance.

And whereas the Company exercifes traffic in this dominion; and, in confequence thereof, her minifters do likewife traffic; and whereas the exercife of traffic is evidently repugnant to a due difcharge

charge of the duties of government, as
being unavoidably productive of deftructive monopolies and oppreſſion ; all which
it is impoſſible to prevent, ſo long as the
Company herſelf ſhall continue a merchant ; be it enacted, that this Company's
commercial charter ſhall be diſſolved ; and
ſhe, and her miniſters, ſhall be reſtrained
from trading or trafficking, directly or indirectly, within the limits of this Indian
dominion, under certain penalties to be
mentioned in a new charter, which ſhall
be granted to this Company, conſtituting
her the United Company of Engliſh Eaſt
India Sovereigns."

Theſe powers, grants, limitations, and
reſtrictions, would have qualified the Company, ſo far as the nature of things could
admit, for adminiſtring the political government ; but, in her military capacity,
as the ſovereign protector, maintainer and
defender of this Indian dominion, ſhe hath
been ſtill leſs qualified, and would therefore have required ſtill more extraordinary
powers. Theſe however we ſhall not ſpe-
cify, as apprehending, that what hath been
already demanded will ſhock. The grant
of ſupreme legiſlative and judicial powers

to

to subjects, over their fellow subjects, must seem an absurd communication of that which is incommunicable: the prohibition of selling and tranferring the shares of stock, would be termed a tyrannical reftraint on private property : the perpetual grant of this sovereignty to the Company, must be deemed an unjuft alienation of the Crown's and Nation's rights: and the diffolution of the Company's commercial charter, would alter her very being and nature. In fhort, if we regard the propofed act fimply, it will appear a collection of abfurd inconfiftencies, and ridiculous nonfenfe : but if we confider it conjunctly with the caufe or purpofe for which it is required, then every abfurdity vanifhes from the act, and centers in the caufe that renders it neceffary. For we appeal to common fenfe, whether every circumftance, fpecified in this propofed act, is not indifpenfably neceffary, to qualify the Company for the fovereign office of adminiftring the political government of this Indian dominion : and, if that neceffity is admitted, then doth the act become a rational and neceffary confequence, of government's having previoufly committed

ted

ted that fovereign charge to the Company. Nay, we muft take the liberty to add, that government, by committing fuch a charge to the Company, and at fame time totally negle&ing to capacitate her for fupporting it, is in a great meafure acceffory to all the ruinous confequences that have enfued from her incapacity.

I am fenfible it will be urged, that we proceed upon falfe premifes, for that government never confidered thefe countries as fubje&ed to the dominion of Britain; that it never granted the fovereignty of them to the Company; nor fuppofed her to be the fovereign; but that it only acquiefced in her holding the Dewanny, on condition of her paying a part of the revenues to the nation; and, of confequence, that government never confidered the inhabitants of thofe countries as fubje&s to the government of Britain. But this is a moft flimfy evafion, like that of fhutting our eyes to the fun, that we may deny it is day: government granted to the Company a right or permiffion to hold the Dewanny; which is explained to be, the power of colle&ing and appropriating the reve-

revenues of Bengal; and, in considera-
tion of this grant, government demanded
and received a fhare of thefe revenues;
government therefore, in its legiflative capacity, admits a knowledge, that the
Company did poffefs the power of collecting, and alfo of applying the revenues of
Bengal, *ad libitum*; and, amongft other
purpofes, to that of defraying the charges
of the military, as well as the civil, government : and government well knows,
that the power which defrays the charges
of the military and civil government, muft
hold the abfolute direction of both : and
what conftitutes fovereign power, but the
abfolute direction of the military and civil
government, together with the difpofal of
the revenues ? But, exclufive of the Dewanny contract, the Company hath applied, in every other characteriftic of a
fovereign, to government, in its legiflative
capacity : fhe hath brought a bill into
parliament, for the grant of certain military powers and indulgences, for the better enabling her to defend, what fhe there
modeftly, though vaguely, terms her territorial acquifitions, (but which, by re-
ferring to the Dewanny contract, is ex-
I   plained

plained to include Bengal :) and she hath
applied for certain juridical powers and
grants, for the better adminiftration of the
jurifdiction, not in her commercial factories, but over the whole country of Bengal : therefore government hath been informed, in its legiflative capacity, by the
Company herfelf, that fhe adminiftred the
military and civil government, and appro-
priated the revenues of Bengal; confequently that fhe was, in every fenfe and
refpect, the actual fovereign of that country.

Now government could not be ignorant
that the Company is a fubject to the national government of Britain ; and that,
as fuch, fhe could have neither right, power, nor force to fubject this dominion, or
afterwards to hold it in fubjection, faving
what fhe derived from the national government; confequently government, as it
underftood that thefe countries were fubjected to the Company, muft have known
that they were fubjected to the dominion
of Britain. And as government did per-
mit the Company to retain this dominion;
and furnifhed her with a military force,
knowing it to be for the purpofe of maintaining

taining dominion, it is plain, that the Company hath held this dominion, no otherwife than by the grant and fupport of government.

But if the Company be the fovereign of Bengal, the inhabitants muft, *per* force, be her fubjects; and if the Company holds this fovereignty as a fubject to the government of Britain, by virtue of the grant or permiffion of that government, and by means of a force furnifhed by the fame government, in what relation can this government regard the inhabitants of Bengal? In that of fubjects furely; tho' the degree hath, by the deed of government, been fomewhat implicated; like' that of a child begot by the father upon his own daughter. And fubjects they have been to the government of Britain, in every fenfe and meaning; they have yielded obedience to thofe fubjects of this government whom it appointed to rule over them; and they have yielded the fruits, as well as the duties of obedience.

But the government of Britain, which hath thus by force fubjected the inhabitants of Bengal to its dominion; which hath, for a feries of years, held them in

fubsubjection; and hath, all along, exacted from them the tribute of subjection; hath withheld from them the protection due to subjects. For it hath scrupulously with-drawn itself from all regard or attention to their government; and hath left it implicitly to the guidance of a few merchants; whom it knew to be perfectly unqualified for administring any sort of government: in consequence of which, these wretched people have, for many years, been ruled, without law, justice, or government. Unhappy subjects, who are forced to obey a sovereign that refuses them protection, and leaves them exposed to all the horrors of tyranny and anarchy.

It will nevertheless be still insisted that government could not, without committing a number of irregularities and absurdities, endow the Company in the manner specified; as also that the Company, when thus endowed, would still have been altogether unequal to the charge of regularly administring a sovereign government. But surely government, if it would not or could not capacitate the Company to regularly govern those countries, ought not to have furnished her the means of oppres-sing, fing, ravaging, pillaging, and ruining them ; to the difgrace of humanity, and the indelible reproach of the Britifh name. Government would have acted a part far more contiftent with the rules of honour and humanity, if, inftead of furnifhing to the Company this military power, it had reitrained her from availing herfelf of the advantage, gained by force and chance, over that mild, unwarlike, but induftrious people ; and obliged her to leave them to their own government.

But then the fituation of affairs in thofe countries, where the nation and Company held fuch a valuable commercial intereft, rendered it highly improper and dangerous to leave the native government to itfelf : moreover the nation and Company could not, in fuch cafe, have acquired the mighty wealth and other benefits that have been derived from the conqueft, or affumed dominion, of thofe countries. Oh wealth, bafely acquired, and foolifhly applied ! Was there then no medium, no middle channel, thro' which government might have fteered the Nation and Company to this fame wealth and benefits, clear of all thefe irregularities, incongruities, inhumanities,

manities, and reproaches? Yes surely;
and one so obvious and confpicuous, that
it is impoffible to conceive how government could be fo induftrious as to fhun or
mifs it. Had the national government
taken upon itfelf the charge of fuperintending the government of thofe countries,
as reafon and the nature of things directed, then would it have furnifhed them a
fovereign, naturally free from all the defects of the Company, and completely
endued with all the qualifications of power, ability, and inclination from intereft,
to protect and regularly govern them.

For it is plain, that the national government, poffeffing fupreme legiflative,
and judicial power, muft have been capable of enforcing obedience to the laws
which it might have enacted for the good
goveriment of thofe countries; and of
punifhing difobedience, not only in the
natives, but in the minifters whom it
would have e nployed to execute that government; as thefe muft have been its
own fubjects. And, on the other hand,
the nation being an immutable body, and
holding this fovereignty in her own right,
and by perpetual tenor; her government

muft

muſt have been actuated, by the ſtrong
motive of ſelf-intereſt, to exert itſelf in
promoting the real and laſting welfare of
thoſe countries. And as to the commercial deſpotiſm, it could never have exiſted
under the national government.

It therefore follows, that the national
government, being perfectly free from all
the defects of the Company, would, by
the ſimple, natural, and rational act of
aſſuming the adminiſtration of government
in thoſe countries, have prevented or reformed all the ſeveral abuſes or evils that
have ſprung from the defective conſtitu-
tion of the Company, as ſovereign. But
beſides the mighty reform of abuſes, that
muſt have been immediately cauſed by thus
changing the perſon of the ſovereign;
there is another advantage, which, though
it cannot be ſaid to ſpring directly from
that change, yet would it have enſued as
a natural conſequence of the national government's taking upon itſelf this ſovereign charge; and that is, the creation or
inſtitution of a new intereſt in that country; a ſort of middle ſtate, betwixt the
native ſubjects and their foreign government.

The

The middle ftate here meant is thd Eaft India Company, (or which is tho fame, her fervants in Bengal ;) which, being now reduced to the condition of a fubject, tho' ftill retaining all her commercial privileges and interefts in that country, would have formed an intermediate link in the political chain, ferving to connect the natives with their government, and government with the natives. For, in every one circumftance that refpected the liberty of the fubject, this middle ftate muft have held precifely the fame intereft as the natives; and, in confequence, the fame inclination to oppofe all oppreffion of government : and, in every thing that refpected the real intereft, the power, or honour of the fovereign, the community of *Natale Solum* muft have led it to fupport the meafures of government. Therefore, this middle ftate, holding a great weight in that dependent dominion, (not indeed from its numbers, but from the powerful fupport and influence of the Company, which would have been ftill very refpectable in the fovereign country,) muft have carried a mighty poife into the fcale of liberty, in oppofition to the defpotifm of government ;

ment; whilst, at same time, it would
have created no danger to the power of the
sovereign. And a middle state of this nature must have been of inexpressible utility; facilitating, in many respects, the establishment of a regular political œconomy
in the government of these countries. For,
in such case, the sovereign could, with
propriety, efficacy, and safety, have conferred every reasonable privilege on the
whole body of subjects in this foreign dominion: seeing that the exertion of these
privileges might have been artfully confined to this middle state : and, as on the one
hand, this finesse would not have, in any
shape, withheld the benefit of these privileges from the natives; but, on the contrary, would have rendered them more
effectually useful to the whole body of subjects, than if they had been committed
either entirely or in common to the natives; because the Company's servants
would, from interest, have had the same
inclination as the natives, to exert these
privileges for the common good; and they
would have had infinitely greater power,
from their superior activity, intrepidity,
and firmness, as also from their superior

K   oppor-

opportunities of obtaining redrefs elfewhere
againft any infringement made by government : fo, on the other hand, the authority of the fovereign could have incurred
no rifk from thefe privileges in the hands
of Europeans ; whereas there is great danger in attempting to confer on the natives
a power to controul even the defpotifm of
government.   With this middle ftate the
power of juries would have been effectual
to the fubject, and harmlefs to the fovereign : however, we fhall have occafion to
be more particular on this head in the
fequel.

But if the national government could,
by taking this fovereign charge upon itfelf, have prevented or reformed thefe many evils and abufes that have arifen from
the defects of the Company ; and could
have likewife created other fuch advantages, facilitating the eftablifhment of a
regular government in thofe countries ;
what reafon can be affigned for government's declining this charge, and devolv-
ing it on the Company ? Government
could not furely fuppofe that this important concern would be managed to greater
national advantage by the Company, than

by

by itfelf: feeing that common fenfe might
have forefeen, what experience hath fince
proved, that, under the management of
the Company, the intereft of Britain in
thofe countries would, in the fpace of a
very few years, be completely annihilated;
that the countries themfelves would either
be completely ruined, or otherwife loft to
enemies; and that the wealth, which was
extorted from them by rapine and general
havoc, being imported into Britain in the
hands of a few indifcreet individuals, would
create a torrent of profufion, extravagance,
luxury, and prodigality, that would fweep
all before it into the gulf of bankruptcy,
perdition, and defpair. Whereas, under
the regular adminiftration of national government, thofe countries might have been
ftill preferved in a flourifhing condition;
and, in confequence, ftill capable of yielding to Britain a tribute little inferior to the
furplus revenue which the Company received in the firft year of the Dewanny:
which tribute, arriving immediately at the
public treafury of Britain, and being there
applied to the diminution of taxes, and
confequent reduction of the price of neceffaries and labour, would have proved a
gentle

gentle univerfal fhower, reviving our de-
cayed and drooping manufactures and
commerce.

But neither could government be indu-
ced to confer this fovereignty on the Company, by any motive of regard to the true
intereft of the proprietors: feeing it was
palpably evident that this charge, being fo
unmeafurably fuperior to her powers of fupporting it, muft unavoidably crufh her to
ruin; and, along with her, the countries
fubjected to her rule; and, it is to be
feared, even that community of which fhe
forms a part. Whereas, if the national
government had taken into its own hands,
and carefully adminiftered the government
of thofe countries, whilft it continued the
Company in poffeffion of her commercial
privileges, fhe would have continued to divide, in the firft place, the fix per cent.
which her commerce, (unaided by revenue)
afforded; even when burdened with the
neceffary expence of a fmall military force
maintained for the guard of that commerce
in thofe foreign countries, and which muft
have been equal to four per cent. on her capital: but this commercial military expence
being rendered in a great meafure unneceffary,

fary, by the immediate protection of national government, the faving thereof would have added two per cent. to her dividend : and the equivalent, which government would have paid for her fortreffes, munition, &c. being added to her capital ftock, would have encreafed her dividend nearly one per cent. more ; whilft her ftock itfelf would, at this day, have been really, and intrinfically worth 220l. inftead of .... its prefent real and intrinfic value.

It would be infulting the underftanding of miniftry, to fuppofe that it had been reftrained from affuming this fovereign charge, by any delicacy of regard to the ideal right of the Company ; derived from either conquefts, as fubjects ; or from the fham grant of a man, who had not power to difpofe of a fingle bega of land, nay, not of a cocoa-nut-tree in that country; and confequently whofe grant of the fovereignty of Bengal could contribute nothing more to inveftiture or poffeffion, than his grant of the crown of Britain could. Though if we fhould (for the fake of argument) fuppofe, that miniftry had really admitted fome fuch right, we muft ftill

esteem

efteem its acquiefcence in that right a moft
abfurd and wildly miftaken indulgence;
feeing it evidently tended to the ruin of
the party whom it meant to favour.

There hath been, however, one weighty argument againft government's affuming
this Indian charge, which is, the danger
arifing to national liberty from government's, (or, in other words, the crown or
miniftry's) acquiring fuch an acceffion of
influence, as muft arife from the poffeffion
of the many emoluments, places, pofts,
&c. annexed to this Indian charge : whereas liberty is completely fecured from fuch
danger, whilft the Company poffeffes it.
And the certainty of this double maxim,
viz. the danger from government's poffeffing this charge, and the fecurity whilft it
is in the hands of the Company, is as generally eftablifhed as almoft any one human principle : for, being violently enforced by thofe whofe perfonal views lead
them to oppofe adminiftration, and at fame
time not fimply allowed, but even inculcated by miniftry itfelf, it hath been readily
credited by thofe who, their perfonal intereft not being fo deeply concerned, were
lefs curious to inveftigate the truth.

It

It may be deemed prefumptuous in an individual, to queftion the orthodoxy of a maxim fo powerfully enforced by one party, readily allowed by the other, and almoft univerfally credited : tho' the extraordinary circumftance, of two violent rival parties concurring fo exactly on a point, where their perfonal intereft feems to be fo materially and fo oppofitely engaged, would lead a byftander to fuppofe, that either one of the two parties muft be miftaken; or otherwife, that one or both muft mifreprefent : at any rate, that uncommon inftance of candour, in miniftry's preaching up a doctrine fo repugnant to that which it pretends to be its own perfonal intereft, would induce fuch byftander to fufpect its fincerity. However, as a right underftanding of this point may confiderably import the public, at this critical juncture, I fhall venture difclofing my fentiments, at the rifk of cenfure for prolixity, as well as impertinence.

With regard to the firft part of the maxim, I conceive that the danger to liberty, from government's holding this charge in its own hands, is fuppofed to arife from the influence which the minifter would acquire,

acquire, over the two fubject branches of
legiflature, (thofe bulwarks of liberty) by
means of the many emoluments, places,
pofts, &c. annexed to the poffeffion of that
charge. But before we admit that the minifters holding this charge would be crea-
tive of that dangerous influence, we ought
to be fatisfied that he doth not already poffefs it, by other means; for, if he doth
already poffefs fuch influence by other
means, it is plain that the Indian charge
cannot confer it; nor will it avail to fhut
one door, whilft there are others open to
admit him. And that the minifter hath
long been in full and plenary poffeffion of
fuch influence, we have ever heard afferted
by thefe very men who fo loudly enforce
the danger of his acquiring it, by means
of this Indian charge: nay, we have much
better authority than their contradictory
affertions, (even that of fact and daily experience,) for believing that the minifter
hath and doth poffefs pofts and places, and
that, on any emergency, he hath in his
power other means equally effectual, towards creating and holding fuch influence, in a degree as plenary and complete as his own heart can defire. And,

if

And, if the minister doth already possess such influence by other means, it is plain, that the Indian charge cannot confer it; nor will it avail to shut one door, whilst there are others open to admit him. And that the minister hath been long in full and plenary possession of such influence, we have ever heard asserted by those very men, who so loudly enforce the danger of his acquiring it, by means of this Indian charge: nay, we have much better authority than their contradictory assertions, (even that of fact and daily experience,) for believing that the minister hath and doth possess posts and places, and that on any emergency he hath in his power other means equally effectual, towards creating and holding such influence, in a degree as plenary and complete as his own heart can desire./ And, if the minister doth already possess an influence so fully sufficient, it must be allowed that, in so much as respects parliamentary influence, this Indian charge would be a thing superfluous and useless to him; like meat to a man that hath already filled his belly; the absence of it can withhold nothing that he wants, and the acquisition cannot

L   confer

confer more than he already poffeffes. I may venture to add, that we certainly hold our liberty by fome latent fecurity, more powerful than that of parliament itfelf, which neither the minifter's in-fluence over parliament, nor pofts and places, will ever induce him to attack, or enable him to fubdue; for that, otherwife, we fhould have been divefted of our pri-vileges and liberty long ago. And, upon confidering thefe feveral circumftances, I conclude, that if this Indian charge was in the hands of government to-morrow, it would neither enable, nor induce the mi-nifter, to attempt a jot more againft our liberty, than he hath done, can do, and will do, without it. However, by way of reinforcing my argument, I fhall add that, if the plan which I mean to pro-pofe fhould be carried into execution, it would leave but few of thefe emolu-ments, &c. to the immediate difpofal of the minifter; and, poffibly, this declara-tion may but little recommend it to his favour.

But ftill, if we were to admit a real danger to liberty from the minifter's pof-feffing thefe emoluments, &c. it remains

to

to be proved that liberty hath been, is,
and will be secured from such danger, by
the Company's holding that Indian charge.
And, when the nature of this security
comes to be examined, I apprehend it will
be found more difficult to prove this latter part of the maxim, than the former.
For it is notorious that, ever until the late
distraction in the Company's affairs, the
arbitrary application of these emoluments,
posts, &c. was vested in the Directors;
and indeed the entire powers and interests
of the Company; insomuch that the Directors might, with propriety, be termed
the Company. So that the whole security of national liberty, and, of course,
the sole obstruction to the minister's dangerous views, depended on the integrity
and independent spirit of 24 Directors;
of whom, again, one or two generally
leads all the rest. Consequently, to come
at the fingering of these dangerous emoluments, &c. the minister had only to
subvert the integrity, or subdue the independance, of these Directors. And, to
effect this, a minister possessed more than
one infallible recipe. By artfully joining
the mighty influence which he held in the

Company's

Company's stock thro' his numerous dependants, to one or other of two parties
contending violently for the direction, he
could reduce both to a perfect dependance
on himself: by the same means he could
hold them in subjection: but still more,
by the awe of wresting from them the
sweet management of this Indian sovereignty, which they were sensible he could
do by a word. And thus he could work
upon their fears. But inclination would
naturally and powerfully lead the Directors to throw themselves into the arms of
a minister; not so much for his immediate assistance; tho' even that might be of
great use, for rendering matters easy with
the proprietors, as well as parliament and
the nation; but because, on these terms,
they secured, in him, an omnipotent sup-
porter and all powerful advocate, against
the day of distress, which they well knew
must come, and that soon: whereas, o-
therwise, they must lay their account
with finding him a severe judge, and bitter prosecutor.

By these several operations on the hopes
and fears of the Directors, it was extremely easy for a minister to render them as
pliant

pliant as a glove; as obedient as a fpaniel, to fetch and carry at bidding, And the Directors being once reduced to this ftate of dependance, it is evident, that the minifter muft poffefs a full and arbitrary power over all the emoluments, pofts, places, &c. appertaining to this Indian charge. But the difpofal of the prefent emoluments, &c. was a trivial matter, compared with other advantages, which this Indian bufinefs, whilft in the hands of the Company, prefented to an artful and enterprifing minifter. For, under the plaufible and indeed undeniable pretext of qualifying the Company for adminiftring this fovereign charge, he might have drawn from the legiflature certain military as well as political powers; which, being gradually augmented as occafion offered, might have at laft eftablifhed a fort of power, in this government, diftinct from and independent of the legiflature: the exertion of which power, being confided to the Directors, would in fact have refted with the minifter. Here indeed was a real danger to liberty; provided it had been poffible to hold up this Indian bufinefs, in the hands of the Company, for

any

any length of time; for, notwithſtanding I conſider national liberty as inexpugnable to the open aſſaults of a miniſter, yet, from ſuch a ſecret convenient and commanding poſt as this mentioned, he might have made frequent ſly and ſuccefsful incurſions on the confines of liberty; which would have greatly ſtraitened her quarters, and waſted her ſtrength.

On the other hand, if that Indian charge had been veſted in the national government, liberty muſt have been perfectly ſecured from this laſt mentioned danger; for, in ſuch cafe, there could have been no pretext for demanding theſe extraordinary diſtinct powers; and, confequently, no opportunity of eſtabliſhing that truly dangerous *imperium in imperio*. And even in the application of the ordinary powers, emoluments, &c. a miniſter muſt have been ſubjected to many troubleſome checks, and reſtraints. His Majeſty, who can have no views diſtinct from the general intereſt of his people, muſt have held a principal voice in every meaſure; as likewiſe muſt ſome others his counſellors. Parliament too muſt have proved an inconvenient reſtraint on a miniſter; particularly

cularly in the article of eſtimates and accounts of revenue, which muſt have been
ſubmitted to its inſpection; and notwithſtanding the certainty of carrying points
by a majority of voices, yet, as there will
ever be ſome refractory members, theſe
might have carried tales to the public;
which, provided this charge had been in
the hands of national government, would
have judged itſelf intereſted in the affair;
and would therefore have taken the liberty to criticiſe his meaſures, or cenſure
his miſconduct. Whereas, this buſineſs
being ſecured, as private property, in the
hands of the Company, king, parliament, and nation were all excluded from
participation: the proprietors alone had a
right to examine meaſures or accounts;
and, the majority of them upon all queſ-
tions being mercenary retainers to mini-
ſtry and the direction, they muſt have ever
been a mere *ſervile pecus.* So that the
buſineſs might have been ſnugly confined
to three or four miniſterial aſſociates,
with their faithful dependants in Leaden-
hall Street; whilſt the miniſter needed
never appear in the affair; free from care,
charge, or trouble; and irreſponſible for
either

[84]

either meafures, or confequences; he might enjoy all the fweets, without the leaft alloy of bitter.

Sure I am if I had been minifter, and minded to make a job of this Indian bufinefs, I would certainly have exerted myfelf moft feduloufly to preferve it in the hands of the Company. And, to divert the nation from ever turning her eye towards it, I would have ftrenuoufly inculcated the rights of the Company, national faith, the impoffibility of conducting this bufinefs otherwife than through the Company; and, above all things, I would, by my emiffaries, have alarmed the public, with fears of danger to their liberty, fhould this bufinefs ever come into the hands of government; whilft, by the fame canal, I would have trumpeted forth my own candour, difintereftednefs as a minifter, indifference to power, and delicate regard to national liberty and private property, in thus difclaiming an object fo replete with minifterial advantages, which was within my power. And thus would I have continued the game, until it was up: and then I would have directed the enquiries, which decency and regard to appearances

extorted

extorted from me, in fuch a manner as to fupprefs, inftead of inveftigating : though, at fame time, I would have boldly expreffed my indignation at the Company's mifconduct; and loudly denounced vengeance againft the individuals that had fhared in the plunder; not a foul that was guilty fhould efcape. And, to wind up the whole affair dextroufly, I would have tafked my own powers, and thofe of my myrmidons, to reprefent all thefe Indian acquifitions as a tranfitory, cafual, and accidental piece of bufinefs; which was altogether out of our tract; and which, if the nation had ever engaged in maintaining them, would have ruined and exhaufted her : and fo the nation was to thank me, for withholding her from ruin.

In this manner, I fay, would I, who am a reptile, have acted, had I been minifter, and minded to make a job of this bufinefs : but I am far from intimating or infinuating that our minifters, who are men of high birth and ftrict honour, could be capable of admitting even a thought of taking fuch bafe advantages.

M   All

All that I have faid is only meant to fhow, that a minifter, if he had the inclination, poffeffed an infinitely fairer opportunity, of converting this bufinefs to finifter purpofes, whilft it was in the hands of the Company ; than he poffibly could have had, from the fame bufinefs, under the conduct of national government. And, from thence, I would infer that, had this bufinefs been in the hands of government, our liberty, nay and our property too, would have been fecured from many dangers, to which they have been expofed, whilft this bufinefs hath been in the hands of the Company.

I cannot then conceive what other objections could be flarted againft government's taking upon itfelf the charge of this Indian dominion : unlefs it be the old trite arguments of timid fluggifh indolence, want of enterprize, &c. That, the diftance of fituation rendering it impoffible for Britain to properly maintain and govern this dominion, it would become an object of no true value or importance, but rather a heavy load exhaufting her ftrength. But it is now more than time for the nation to recal her faith from men whom

whom fhe hath fufficient ground to fufpect of deceit; and, roufing her fenfes, to take the liberty of trying thefe matters by the ftandard of her own reafon; which we fhall endeavour to aid by the following hints.

To properly demonftrate the true value and importance of this Indian dominion to Britain, would demand a volume; we have, in the firft part, prefented a flight fketch of it; here therefore we fhall offer only one or two remarks refpecting its importance to our finances; and though we do not offer thefe remarks as the refult of exact calculation, yet will they ferve to throw a light on this fubject. Ever fince the laft war Britain hath paid annually to foreign creditors, in intereft, about 1,500,000 l. and this is paid, not in paper, but all in hard money; or, otherwife, in what is equivalent, the ftoppage of fo much hard money as is reckoned to come into Britain by the balance of her trade. On the other hand, the net fpecie balance of trade with all the world, (exclufive of that part which ftrictly and properly may be termed the produce of Indian dominion,) after de-

ducting

ducting the imperceptible and enormous
drain of specie made by smuggling, doth
not at this day perhapsamount to 800,000l.
The difference then betwixt her numerical
specie disburfement and receipt in balance
of trade, muft needs have been made good
from fome other fund than the circulating
ftock of fpecie, otherwife circulation muft
in that number of years have totally ceafed.
And this fund we need not mention to
have been the dominion in India. Ever
fince 1757, the private fortunes acquired
there in confequence of dominion or conqueft, having been remitted either in bills
on foreign Indian companies, or in dia-
monds, have created an annual influx of
fpecie, (or what is equivalent,) to the a-
mount of at leaft 700,000 l. * The Company

* As it is impoffible to exactly afcertain the annual
amount of this private remittance made through various channels, it will no doubt be alledged, that we
have exaggerated this article ; and yet we have certain
ground to affirm, that it is greatly underrated.
Sure I am, if we can fuppofe that the amount of
fuch remittance made from 1757 to 1770 hath been in
any degree equal to that of the two following years,
(which is afcertained,) and we have no reafon to fuppofe that there hath been any confiderable difference,
the

pany too received since that period, and previous to the Dewanny, though by virtue of dominion or conquest, sundry large sums of money; which she invested in merchandize; and, thereby, saved to Britain so much specie as she would, otherwise, have transmitted for the purchase of such merchandize; and it doth not require demonstration to prove, that all such saving is, in every respect, the same as the influx

the sum assigned by us will be greatly under mark. For no sooner did the English Company, in 1770, open her treasury, to receive money for remittance to Britain, than there was poured in at her three capital settlements above 1,400,000 l. for which bills were granted, presented, and accepted by the Company, and nearly two thirds of this sum was borrowed in Bengal, And in 1771 she hath borrowed in Bengal alone, under the promise of remittance, a sum perhaps exceeding the whole loan of the former year; though the bills have been postponed by her agents in Bengal, on account of the Company's inability to answer them. Such was the remittance of British private fortunes for these two years, through the channel of the English Company alone: and we have good reason to suppose, that there may have been some made through other channels. And these enormous sums, borrowed by the Company, as sovereign, for the expence of Bengal, in these two years, will serve to show the mighty alteration of affairs in that country since 1765.

influx of an equal fum. And ever from 1765, till fome time in 1770, the Company paid for all her cargoes, not only in India but in China, with the furplus revenue of Bengal: and of courfe this furplus revenue hath, for that fpace, faved, (which is the fame as gained) annually to Britain, the whole fums which the Company ufed to tranfmit for the purchafe of her cargoes in India and China; and which, on an average, may be reckoned 500,000 l. *per annum:* but thefe cargoes were, from 1765, encreafed to an enormous degree; and if we add only 200,000l. for fuch encreafe, we fhall find that the furplus revenue of Bengal hath, by the return of trade, created an annual influx to Britain of at leaft 700,000 l. in fpecie: and this, added to the private fortunes, makes 1,400,000 l. received yearly by Britain, from Indian dominion.

But, for thefe two years paft, the ruinous fituation of thofe countries, and the confequent deficiency of revenue, hath obliged the Company to either tranfmit money from Europe, or otherwife to borrow money abroad, on bill or bond, for the purchafe of all her cargoes in India as well

well as China: and the Company, by thus borrowing, for the purchase of cargoes, and even the expence of her government, hath abforbed the private fortunes, which, till then, had been tranfmitted to Britain, by bills on foreign companies. We muft therefore perceive, without defcending to tedious inveftigation, that the ruined ftate of thofe countries, having cut off furplus revenue, hath, for thefe two years paft, diminifhed the annual influx to Britain from Indian dominion, at leaft one half, or 700,000 l. And this diminution of influx, whilft our drain continues the fame, we already begin to feel in our circulation : though this felt effect is not yet traced up to its caufe. Of what mighty importance then muft this Indian dominion have been, to the circulation of Britain : when this circulation feels feverely, from only two years partial deprivation of the benefit formerly derived from that dominion ? And what effect muft a total deprivation of that benefit operate, in a few years, on this circulation; whilft, we are continuing to pay to our foreign creditors about 1,500,000 l. *per annum* in numerical fpecie; exclufive of other lefs
noted

noted drains, which, it is moft probable mount it up much higher? And yet it is evident, that Britain muft, unavoidably, be deprived of this whole benefit, fo foon as fhe fhall lofe her dominion in India; whether that lofs fhall be caufed by enemies, or by the ruin of the countries fubjected. Nay, by lofing the dominion of Bengal fingly, fhe muft not only incur a deprivation of almoft the whole dominion benefit; but fhe muft likewife lofe by far the moft valuable part of that commerce, which was carried on by the Company with thofe countries, previous to dominion. For the commerce with Bengal, alone, is of much greater value, than that with all the reft of India: and, as to the trade with China, it is the moft pernicious and lofing trade to the nation; however convenient it may be to government.

And if we fhall then advert to the benefit and fupport which the finances of Britain have received from this Indian dominion, for fo many years paft, though under the moft prepofterous management; but, ftill more, if we fhall advert to the nature and degree of benefit that, under proper management, might have been derived

derived *in perpetuum* from this Indian dominion, in not only the article of finance,
but in other weighty refpects : and, if we
fhall, yet farther, look forward to the
difmal confequences that muft unavoidably enfue to Britain, in thefe feveral refpects, from a deprivation of this Indian
dominion and its benefits; can we tamely
furrender our reafon to the *ipfe dixit* of men
who are hardy enough to tell us, that Indian dominion is of no value nor utility
to Britain:

Nor do thefe men lefs abufe our underftanding, by holding forth the difficulty of
maintaining and defending this dominion :
feeing that, of all nations in the world,
Britain is, by a variety of circumftances,
the beft qualified to maintain and defend
maritime or commercial dominion in India. For, as fhe exceeds all the world in
naval force, fhe is, through that circumftance alone, the moft capable of defending fuch dominion, againft the affault of
European enemies : and had Britain availed
herfeif of evident advantages, had fhe
eftablifhed her naval and land defence upon
the plan that fhall be explained, Britifh
dominion in India might, at this day, have
been fecured from even the attempt of

European

European rivals : they might have admired and envied, but they would not have dared to attack. And thefe European rivals are the only dangerous enemies to Britifh dominion in India : for as to the neighbouring native powers, they would, from fear as well as inclination, have been amicable to Britain ; provided her government in thofe countries had acted with common honefty, and common decorum, or prudence ; and not as common robbers. And, as to the unhappy native fubjects themfelves, their loyalty hath been fufficiently proved, by fo many years patient fubmiffion to the moft intolerable of all poffible governments. Wherein then confifts the difficulty of maintaining and defending Britifh dominion in India ?

And with regard to the fo much talked of expence or drain of native ftrength, we may furely, with good reafon, fay that this objection militated much ftronger againft maintaining that dominion under the Company, than under national government : tho' the nature and extent of even that drain under the Company, is moft grofsly mifreprefented. For I am well informed that the Company's annual recruit, fince the time fhe completed her dominion force,

hath

hath never exceeded 1200 men ; and I am afraid it hath in general fallen fhort of 1000; notwithftanding fhe laboured under many difadvantages, from which national government would be exempted : fuch as being obliged to put up with very indifferent and unhealthy recruits, for want of better; too little attention paid to the manner of tranfporting them ; and ftill lefs to their health and manner of living in the country : whilft her governors expended numbers of them on unneceffary predatory wars. And even this recruit we are not to reckon a drain of real ftrength from Britain : feeing that the Company's recruits have been moftly fellows of the moft defperate circumftances, who had no means of fubfifting at home ; and who therefore would, if the Company had not taken them off, have been taken off by the gallows, or otherwife would have emigrated to America or fome other country, in fearch of bread ; and would thus have been equally loft to Britain. So that, upon rationally confidering this matter, we fhall find that, for the maintenance of dominion in India, the Company hath not drained this country, of 100 men annually,

nually, that could, in any fenfe, be termed ufeful, or a real ftrength to it. But,
fetting afide the precedent of the Company, it is certain that, to maintain and
defend the mighty dominion of Bengal,
demands an European force very little fuperior in number to the garrifon of that
barren fortrefs Gibraltar : and to maintain
and defend the whole territorial poffeffions,
together with the commerce of Britain in
India, requires a force very little exceeding the aforefaid garrifon with that of its
fifter fortrefs in Minorca. And the annual
recruit, neceffary to keep up this force,
after allowing largely for climate, and
every other circumftance, would, on a
complete plan of defence, not exceed 900
or at moft 1000 men : and, of this recruit,
at leaft 200, would be wanted annually
to maintain commerce, if there was no
dominion. Nay, if this is judged too
great a drain for Britain, one fourth part
of that number may be reduced, by re-
cruiting that proportion of foreign pro-
teftants : fuch being eafily procured ; and,
in fuch a low proportion, they can in no
refpect be dangerous. And can Britain
regard 6 or 700 men annually as too great
a drain

a drain, for the maintenance of that important dominion and commerce, which is as one of the capital limbs of her body; and at fame time beftow a nearly equal fhare of her ftrength on maintaining thefe two barren, and I had almoft faid ufelefs, fortreffes; the pecuniary charge of which fhe pays out of her proper finance, never to return; whilft Indian dominion defrays its own charge.

The only remaining objection then to Indian dominion is, the difficulty of properly governing it. But this difficulty doth not arife, like that in America, from the indomitably obftinate fpirit of the fubjects; on the contrary, it arifes from their over paffive or fubmiffive difpofition, and incapacity of refifting the power of government: and this, inftead of being an objection, is the moft valuable qualification of a dependent dominion. To remove this difficulty demands no exterior aids, no exertion of powers or force; it depends entirely on the will of the fovereign; and a very little art, a very little care, with a little honefty, would ferve to completely remedy it; as we doubt not to evince.

In

In fine, Bengal, being one of the richeft commercial countries is, to Britain as
a commercial nation, the nobleft and moft
truly valuable acquifition that providence
could poffibly beftow on her : by the mild
difpofition of its inhabitants it is the moft
facily governed and maintained; and, by
the nature of its fituation, it is the moft
defenfible foreign dominion on this globe;
particularly to Britain which excels in
naval force. And one may almoft venture to fay that providence, by throwing
Bengal into the arms of Britain, feems to
have intended that this, the richeft commercial ftate in Afia, which, through the
effeminacy of its inhabitants, is incapable
of maintaining its own independance,
fhould be fubjected to Britain, as being
the fitteft, through fimilarity of commercial difpofition, intereft, and modes,
to properly govern it; and, through her
fuperiori y in naval force, the beft qualified to defend and protect it from all
enemies.

In what light then muft pofterity
regard the policy of Britain, during
the third quarter of the eighteenth cen-
tury : when it fhall find her, in the Eaft,
flighting

flighting and giving up that glorious field,
which annually-yielded a golden crop, to
be rutted up and trodden down by hogs
and viler beafts : whilft, in the Weft, fhe
was tugging with all her might, exerting
her utmoft ftudy, care and attention, much
ftrength, and more money, on cultivating
the fea fands; ftraining to fubdue nature;
and forcing the horfe to drink in fpite of
inclination ? Will it not be faid, that fhe
would have acted a far wifer part, if fhe had
left nature and time to flowly operate in
America, the effects which they will unavoidably produce, in fpite of all her ef-
forts; and had converted her care and attention, to properly govern, and maintain,
that noble, rich, and grateful dependent
dominion in India; which, upon fuch
terms, would have poured, into her pub-
lick treafury, refources, that would have
ferved to alleviate her burden of taxes;
and, confequently, to reduce the price of
neceffaries, of labour, and of manufactures; which, again, would have preferved her commerce, not only with America, but with other countries; and would
at fame time have preferved to her thou-
fands of induftrious and ufeful fubjects,
who,

who, through want of employment, were forced to emigrate from her to America. And, by the fame care and attention to the government and revenue of that Indian dominion, fhe would have prevented the inundation of eaftern profufion and extravagance; which chiefly contributed to convert this formerly graniferous ifland, into a pafture for horfes of parade and ftately pride; infomuch that, inftead of fupplying her neighbours as formerly, with fome hundred thoufand pounds worth of grain annually, fhe could not feed the greatly reduced number of her own inhabitants; nor furnifh the means of living to the induftrious agricultor, and peafant; who, in fearch of livelihood, fled from her to America; thereby debilitating her own beft fource of ftrength, and prematurely accelerating the manhood of thofe otherwife infant colonies.

Neverthelefs there ftill remains a poffibility of retrieving this error in policy; or at leaft of preventing a farther encreafe of the evils that have arifen from it; provided that, in the firft place, this Indian dominion fhall ftill be in our poffeffion: and, in the fecond place, that national govern-

government shall, by taking upon itself
the charge of adminiftring the government thereof, remedy that firft and radical caufe of evil and abufe which hath
exifted under the Company's government :
and fhall, at fame time, with honeft and
fincere intention, fpirit and activity, apply a proper remedy to that which hath
been affigned as the fecond caufe of evil,
and the nature of which remedy fhall be
explained in the fequel. For, upon fuch
terms, there is no doubt that a regular
fyftem of government may be eftablifhed
in that dependent dominion ; under which
it may be reftored to its priftine profperity, nay, it may be elevated to a ftate ftill
more flourifhing than it ever knew; and,
in confequence, to a capacity of yielding
a ftill fuperior degree of benefit to Britain ;
and in a manner widely different, and true-
ly falutary to her.

But I muft again repeat, that it is vain
to expect this reform of evils from the
management of the Company ; loaded as
fhe is with fo many natural defects, which
it is out of the power of art to remedy,
otherwife than by conferring upon her the
fovereign government of Britain, along

O   with

with that of this dependent dominion. For the execution of thefe two fovereign governments is, by the nature of things, infeparable : it being morally impoffible, that any power can execute the fovereign government of thofe Indian countries, as a dominion dependent upon Britain, unlefs that power fhall poffefs the fovereign execution of government in Britain.

However, it would be ftill more vain to look for any good from that extravagant fancy of joining the Company, with government, in this fovereign charge. What quota of powers, proper to her and wanting to government, can the Company contribute, to render her a neceffary or ufeful affociate with government, in this fovereign charge ? I doubt not that the propofer's intentions were good and honeft : but his fcheme would be fo far from promoting his or any one good purpofe, that it would produce the very oppofite effects. For, inftead of checking and contrafting, it would ferve, in the firft place, to furnifh, in the Directors and their governors, a convenient cloke of excufe to miniftry and its governors, with the nation ; whilft miniftry and its governors would ferve the Direc-

tors

tors and their governors a like good turn
with the proprietors : they would mutually vouch for and fcreen each other ; neither would be refponfible, and neither
would act ; and thus, between ftools, &c.
in the fecond place, commercial defpotifm which, by feparating the Company
from the powers of government and the
confequent jealoufy of privilege, muft have
been completely fuppreffed, would, under
this double-headed monfter, flourifh with
redoubled vigour : the national governors
would, by their connection with the Company's, become merchants as well as tyrants ; and the Company's governors
would, by their power in the government,
continue tyrants as well as merchants : and
thus the candle would burn at both ends.
In the third place, the Company which,
by being excluded from the powers of government, would have contributed fo ef-
fentially in the nature of a middle ftate to
the eftablifhment of a regular political fyftem in thofe countries, muft, by being
joined in the execution of government, entirely lofe that virtue : inftead of fupporting liberty, fhe would join in promoting
tyranny ; and would ftill continue a ruin-

ous

ous peft to thofe countries. Indeed that ftrange partnerfhip of Nation and Co. in this fovereignty bufinefs, is a cure infinitely worfe than the difeafe.

In fhort, there is no alternative : if Britain means to preferve the poffeffion of that mighty benefit derived from dominion and commerce in India; if fhe means to prevent the abfolute ruin of the Company, and her creditors; if fhe hath any regard to the loud cry of oppreffion fent forth to her for a feries of years, by her numerous wretched fubjects in thofe countries; and means to fave them from final deftruction, fhe muft furnifh their government with a fovereign, or head, properly qualified to adminifter it : for this is the foundation, as well as the crowning of all good government; it is the center upon which the machine revolves, from which every line iffues, and in which every line terminates; it is the *fine qua non*, for without it no regular government can exift. And what proper fovereign can Britain furnifh to that dependent dominion, unlefs it be her own fovereign government ?

We have fhown that the nation and her fupreme government are perfectly equal to
the

the charge: to them there is not the
fmalleft difficulty in fupporting it. Neither is there the fmalleft difficulty to her
executive government or miniftry, provided it fhall poffefs an ordinary fhare of fpirit, activity, or enterprize; and fhall proceed with fincere and upright intention.
For, a regular form of government being
once eftablifhed abroad, and a properly
digefted office or department formed at
home, the bufinefs would go on with great
fmoothnefs and facility to miniftry.

Neverthelefs, as I have affumed the liberty of prefcribing in this important and
almoft defperate cafe, I am forry, that a fincere regard to the welfare of the patient
fhould compel me to add, (by way of con-
cluding on this head,) that, unlefs miniftry fhall act upon a principle, and with a
fpirit, extremely different from that which
it hath hitherto difcovered in this bufinefs,
it would be much more advifeable to continue the charge in the hands of the Company: for it can be but ruined under her.
However, in ftrong hopes of a melioration
in thefe refpects, which depends altogether
on the will of government, I fhall proceed

to

to difclofe that plan, which, in the hands
of a properly qualified fovereign, would, I
doubt not, ferve to eftablifh a regular fyftem
of government in India.

A PLAN,

FOR

ESTABLISHING A REGULAR SYSTEM

OF

POLITICAL GOVERNMENT

IN

I N D I A.

WE have before obferved, that the
fecond caufe why thefe reftraining
and impelling powers, which alone can
prevent tyranny and anarchy, have been altogether wanting in the Company's fyftem
of government, appears to be the diftance
of fituation, betwixt the fovereign refidence and the country governed. And we
fhall here add that, if national government fhould adopt the fame fyftem, this
diftance

diſtance would operate, under it, effects
the ſame in nature as theſe under the Company; and nothing but the difference in
other circumſtances, betwixt the national
government and Company, could prevent
theſe effects from being likewiſe equal in
degree. For it is evident that, if the executive government of the nation ſhould, as
the Directors have done, preſerve to itſelf
the charge and power of immediately ſu-
perintending and controuling the execution
of government in that Indian dominion,
the diſtance of ſituation would create to
that government an equal impoſſibility of
adviſing and directing meaſures, of en-
forcing the execution or obſervance of orders, and of preventing or reſtraining abuſe:
conſequently, in the immediate execution
of all meaſures, the national governors
would poſſeſs the ſame unlimited power, as
the Company's governors have done. And
the only advantage to that Indian government, from national governments aſſuming
from the Company the charge of adminiſtring it, would ariſe from the following
circumſtances. Firſt, the ſuperior retroſpec-
tive or *ex poſt facto* authority of national
government, enabling it to judge and pu-
niſh

nith the maladminiftration, or difobedience of its minifters. Second, The fuperior inclination or difpofition of national
government (arifing from its perpetual intereft in the property) to exert itfelf in
promoting proper meafures. Third, The
fuppreffion of commercial defpotifm. And
fourth, The exiftence of the Company as
a middle ftate betwixt the natives and their
foreign government. All which innova-
tions, arifing from national government's
taking upon itfelf the adminiftration of
this Indian government, though they are
indifpenfably neceffary and highly condu-
cive to the eftablifhment of a regular political fyftem, yet do we perceive that they,
fingly and unfupported, cannot fuffice to
create that due proportion of reftraint on
the power, or of impulfe on the will of the
deputed executive government, which is
abfolutely neceffary to the perfect fuppreffion of tyranny, anarchy, and abufe. Nor
is it poffible to complete this reftraint and
impulfe, to that fufficing degree, unlefs by
a proper exertion of the fovereign's own
fupreme influence.

But we find that, upon the Company's
fyftem, the diftance of fituation renders
the.

the influence of the sovereign altogether
impotent to this effect: and if we should
take it for granted that her system hath
been just or complete, then must we conclude, that this sovereign impotence is a
consequence naturally and unavoidably a-
rising from the distance; and, therefore,
above the remedy of art. But, if we
consult our own reason, we shall perceive
that the Company's impotence, in that
particular respect, proceeded from a radical defect or error in her system; which
might have been remedied by art. For,
it is evident, that the distance of situation
was in every circumstance similarly and
equally obstructive to the Company's immediately or personally executing the government of that Indian dominion, as it
was to her immediately restraining or en-
forcing the manner of execution: and yet
we find that the Directors could discover
a remedy for the first of these obstruc-
tions, by the succedaneum of appointing
a deputed executive government. And, as
the second sprung from the same cause,
and was exactly similar in its nature, common sense must surely have instructed her,
that it was to be removed by a similar re-

P   medy,

medy : it being certain that, if the Directors had thought proper to inftitute in India a deputation properly qualified to controul their executive deputation, the meafures of thofe Indian governments might have been enforced or reftrained by the fovereign refiding in Europe, as effectually as they have been executed by the fame fovereign : that is to fay, as effectually, as the defective conftitution of the Company, (which equally difqualified her for controuling as for executing,) could admit.

But it could not be ignorance, or want of common fenfe, that prevented the Directors from inftituting a controuling deputation of this nature : feeing they had before them the precedent of thefe other European nations, who hold any poffef-fions in India : all of whom have provided fomething of this kind : for inftance, the Dutch government at Batavia. Sound policy quickly pointed out to the Dutch, the abfurdity of committing the charge of their difperfed concerns in India, to a multiplicity of diftinct heads, all acting under no other conftraint, or reftraint, than that of the Company's Directors refiding in Europe.

Europe. Therefore, fo foon as the Dutch Company began to extend her poffeffions in India, fhe inftituted one fupreme government at Batavia, with full powers, and authority, to direct and controul the executive government of all her other fettlements. And this government acts in India as an intermediate power, betwixt the Company refiding in Europe, and her various poffeffions in that diftant country; and as the perpetual refidentiary fupervifor of all her interefts there. The Directors communicate all their purpofes immediately to it : and it difperfes orders and inftructions to all the fubordinate governments ; which again tranfmit to it a regular account of their fituation, wants, or tranfactions. All governors, chiefs, &c. are immediately refponfible to it : all appointments to, and removals from, office in the fuborninates, are made immediately by it : and all complaints or appeals, againft the mifconduct or injuftice of thefe governors, are immediately addreffed to it. In fine, it may be termed the center of the Dutch government in India. And though this government can in no fhape be, termed the complete model of a deputation, fit

to

to controul or enforce the execution of
fovereign government, in various territorial
dominions; yet, to this inftitution, defective as it is, the Dutch owe it, that
the government of their numerous fubordinate poffeffions in India hath been con-
ducted, for about two hundred years,
clear of any enormous abufe.

But if the Dutch and other European
nations, which hold little other concern
in India than a few fettlements eftablifhed
there for the purpofe of commerce, found
it neceffary, for the regular management
of thefe commercial concerns, to inftitute a fort of intermediate fupreme power,
as a local check on the reft of their fettlements: how much more incumbent
was it on the Englifh Company, to conftitute an immediate directing and controuling power, over the conduct of her deputies, who were entrufted with the charge
of executing the fovereign government,
of fundry mighty ftates; a charge of fuch
fuperior intricacy, weight, importance,
and delicacy; and fo very liable to be
abufed.

What may have been the motive of the
Directors for thus wilfully omitting an inftitution

ftitution fo evidently ufeful and neceffary,
I fhall not pretend to determine. Poffibly they might apprehend that if, upon
their acquiring this mighty fovereign dominion, they fhould alter that which had
been all along their commercial fyftem,
fuch alteration might induce the nation
to enquire into the caufe of it, and fo difcover the nature of their dominion, which
they have ever carefully hid from the public. Though, it is more probable, they
might perceive, that the inftitution of fuch
an intermediate power would greatly interfere with their own perfonal influence,
power, and emoluments ; feeing it muft
have poffeffed the immediate difpofal of
places and pofts, as well as a confiderable
fhare in the direction of affairs : and, in
order to prevent this, they preferved to
themfelves the power, of immediately fuperintending, and directing, the execution of government in thofe Indian dominions.

But whatever the motive of the Directors may have been, it is certain, that
the want of a deputed controuling power
in India, hath been a radical and grievous
defect in their fyftem : which hath produced

duced a number of thofe evils that have
been falfely afcribed to the diftance of fituation. And though we are far from al-
ledging, that it was poffible for the Company to eftablifh in thofe countries a government in any degree regular, feeing that
the numerous natural defects in her conftitution, unavoidably producing many
deftructive abufes, muft have ever proved an infuperable obftacle to that; yet
do we affirm that, the inftitution of a
duly qualified intermediate controuling
power, would have totally prevented fome,
and would have greatly diminifhed moft,
of thefe enormous abufes which, upon
the fyftem of the Directors, have ferved
to ruin thofe countries.

Now we have feen that the national government would, by taking upon itfelf
the charge of adminiftring that Indian
government, remedy or fupprefs all the
abufes that have fprung from the defective
conftitution of the Company, (befides
creating other circumftances of high utility, that could not exift under the Company's government.) And as the diftance
of fituation, preventing the fovereign from
immediately exerting his fupreme influence

over

over the deputed executive government, is the only remaining caufe of evil or abufe; it is plain that, if it is poffible to conftruct in India, a deputed power, upon fuch principles, as that it fhall effectually and completely fupply the place of the fovereign, in immediately directing, en-forcing, and controuling the meafures of the deputed executive government, then muft the only obftruction to the eftablifh-ment of a regular political fyftem, be re-medied and removed. Confequently the grand *defideratum*, the only thing that is wanting, to enable the national govern-ment of Britain to regularly adminifter the government of thofe Indian dominions, is the inftitution of a deputed controuling power in India, properly qualified to ful-fil the purpofes that have been here fpe-cified.

And that it is poffible, to conftitute an intermediate power in India, that fhall effectually and faithfully direct, enforce, and controul the meafures of the deputed executive government in thofe Indian do-minions, I doubt not to evince: though, at fame time, I am fully fenfible of the many real difficulties, arifing from nature

and

and circumftance, to obftruct it; as likewife of the many artificial difficulties pro-
ceeding from the endeavours of thofe
who have an intereft to obftruct fuch a
meafure; and who have influence to enforce their objections, however futile, on
the underftanding of others.

But before we proceed to defcribe the
plan upon which we mean to conftruct
this controuling deputation, it will be neceffary to explain the extent of its charge,
or number of the government's compofing that dominion which it is meant to
controul. For tho', in our defcription of
the Company's government in India, we
confined our account to that of Bengal
alone, as being the moft important and
beft known part of her dominion; yet
doth the Company poffefs, befides Bengal, certain other territorial governments,
of no fmall value and importance, in refpect of either revenue or commerce. All
which governments being formed upon
the fame fyftem as that of Bengal, do not
lefs demand reform, fupervifion, and controul.

For, in the firft place, the government
of Madrafs poffeffes a very confiderable
and

and valuable territorial dominion, avowedly in the name and right of the Company. This same government doth likewise, in every thing beside the name, possess the absolute sovereignty of that rich commercial province of Arcot, or the Carnatic, in which it is situated : for, notwithstanding it tolerates a nominal Nabob, whose name it uses in most acts of government ; and who, consequently, for the Company's convenience, possesses the shadow of sovereignty ; yet, as the government of Madrass holds the charge of defending the country, and maintains the military force requisite thereto, it is the actual sovereign : seeing that, in all Indian or Asiatic governments, he who holds the sword must be the absolute lord and master. And, notwithstanding all the Company's parade of appearances, this Nabob of Arcot is, in respect of sovereign power, as much a pageant as he of Bengal : a mere screen or blind, placed before the Company's sovereignty.

Bombay is likewise embarked in dominion, since it seized on the rich commercial city of Surat, with its district, &c. Though sound policy must direct Britain

Q

to reprobate all territorial dominion on that fide of the peninfula; as caufing a dangerous divifion and weakening of her force and defence.

But the fame policy will inftruct Britain to regard dominion on the eaft fide of that peninfula in an oppofite light; becaufe, on that fide lay all the truly valuable dominions which fhe already poffeffes.

To fully explain what is the true intereft of Britain, refpecting territorial dominion in India, would be, here, foreign and tedious; and, to flightly touch on that fubject, might afford ground for cenfure and criticifm: we fhall only obferve, in the general, that Britain ought to value only fuch dominion in India as is maritime: becaufe, in the firft place, thefe are ever trading and manufacturing countries; and, as fuch, are highly ufeful to her proper commerce; they are likewife capacitated, by their own active foreign trade, to richly reimburfe her for her expence of native ftrength in defending them, as well as for her trouble in governing them: and, in the fecond place, being acceffible to her naval force, they are eafily maintained and defended by her. Therefore, fo much
of

of this maritime dominion as she can maintain and defend, without creating any additional expence of native strength; and, upon a footing so connected with that truly valuable dominion which she already possesses, as not to cause any dangerous division of that original strength, so much of this maritime dominion in India may be truly useful and advantageous to her; on any other terms it may be detrimental.

Such is the present state of British dominion in India : and such is the interest of Britain, with respect to future augmentation of dominion in that country. And we have undertaken to plan the construction of an intermediate power or deputation, which, under the national government of Britain, shall effectually and faithfully superintend, enforce, and controul the measures of these several governments that, at present are, or in future may be, subjected to Britain : and which deputation shall of course, in the first place, enable the national government of Britain to establish a regular system of political government over this whole present or future dominion : and, in the second place, shall constitute a complete system of

Q 2   military

military government, and fecure defence, for all the feveral branches of this dominion. At prefent we are on the fubject of political government.

The properties requifite to qualify this intermediate power, or deputation, for effectually fuperintending, enforcing, and controuling the political government of dominion in India, are, firft, virtue and integrity, to faithfully and honeftly difcharge the duties of its office: and, fecond, power or ability, to effectually fulfil the purpofe of its inftitution. The latter is more eafily conferred; but the former is rendered difficult, by fundry obftructions, arifing from the nature or difpofition of the perfons who muft necef-farily be employed to compofe this deputation. For it is needlefs to obferve, that this controuling power cannot be lodged in the fubjects native of the dependent dominion; the nature of the government, as well as the nature of their difpofition, rendering that impracticable; (as hath been fhewn): otherwife this difficulty might be more eafily furmounted. But, the Indian fubjects being fet afide, there remains no choice; this controuling deputation muft,

per

per force, be compofed of Britifh born fubjects : whilft the feveral governments, which it is meant to controul, are at fame time executed by Britifh born fubjects. And, from this circumftance, it follows, that the perfonal intereft of the party controuling muft naturally be the very fame, with that of the party controuled : and, of courfe, the views of both muft likewife be the fame.

This fimilarity or famenefs of perfonal intereft and views it is that creates the difficulty of conferring virtue, integrity, honour, and fidelity, on the controuling deputation. For it is morally certain, that the fimilarity of intereft and views will, naturally and invariably, draw the party controuling, to concur and join, inftead of controuling or oppofing, the meafures of the party executing, (feeing fuch meafures tend to promote that which is their common intereft) provided that this party controuling fhall poffefs the power, and opportunity of fo joining intereft, with the party executing. And it is no lefs certain, that this controuling deputation muft, unavoidably, poffefs the opportunity of thus joining interefts, unlefs it can,

by

by some means, be prevented and reftrained from joining and uniting the action of
its own proper powers, with the action of
thefe powers that are proper to the executive office. Whereas, if it fhall be
found poffible to divide and feparate the
action of thefe two different powers, the
one from the other, in a manner fo diftinct, that each fhall act, in the fphere affigned to it, with freedom and liberty; and
neither fhall have the opportunity of tranfgreffing the limits prefcribed, to its own
proper department, by the fovereign;
then, and in fuch cafe, it is not only poffible, but certain, that this controuling
deputation may, and will be, prevented
from joining interefts, with the executive
deputation; and, confequently, from promoting the very meafures which it was
meant to reftrain. And, from thence I
conclude, that the only poffible and certain
means of conferring, on this controuling
deputation, virtue and integrity to faithfully
and honeftly difcharge the duties of its
office, is to cut it off from all opportunity of joining the powers of its office,
with thofe of the executive; or of affuming any fhare in the executive government:

ment : in other words, it muft be reftrained from interfering, either directly or indirectly, perfonally or by proxy, in the
immediate execution of meafures, in any
one of thefe governments which it is meant
to controul.

But it is evident that, if this controuling deputation fhall exift or refide within
any one of thofe dominions whofe government it is meant to controul, it will
be morally impoffible to prevent it from
joining its powers, and, confequently, its
interefts, views, and meafures, with the
deputed executive power of that government where it refides. For, by virtue of
its authority, which from the nature of
its office muft needs be fupreme over the
executive deputation, it will ufurp at leaft
a part if not the whole power of execution : or otherwife it will, by confent, join
and unite its powers with thofe of the executive, in order to promote their mutual
intereft, by meafures diametrically repugnant to the purpofe of its inftitution. Nor
is it poffible, in this cafe, by any art, device or feparation into parts, to prevent
this ufurpation or union : let the controuling power be termed judges, fupervifors,
officers

officers of the revenue, or what elfe; and
let the office of controuling be divided,
into as many parts as can be conceived;
ftill, the difference of term, will not
alter the nature of the men employed; nor will the divifion of parts feparate their intereft. All the various perfons, compofing this office, will ftill be Europeans; the fame as thefe who compofe
the executive office; and fo, all the perfons in both offices will be foreign to the
country governed, acting by an authority
which is deputed mutable and temporary;
confequently they will all hold the fame
view; which is, to amafs all the money
they can during the fhort term of their
office, in order to tranfport it to their
own country: and as all of them would,
by virtue of their refiding within the fame
government, poffefs the fame powers, and
the fame opportunities of exerting them,
they would all be irrefiftably attracted, by
the omnipotent fympathy of felf-intereft,
to join their feveral powers, in promoting
that which is the common view of one
and all of them. In fine, if thefe controuling and executive deputations, which
thus, from the community of the *natale*
folum,

folum, hold one and the fame intereft, fhall both refide together in one and the fame government, and thereby poffefs the fame opportunities, it will be equally impoffible to prevent thefe two deputations, however artfully feparated into parts, from joining and uniting their different powers, &c. as it is to preferve feparate the guttæ of quickfilver; which, however gently and carefully they are dropt upon the fame confined and fmooth furface, will meet, join, and conglobate into one united mafs. But if the controuling deputation fhall be thus permitted to join its powers with thefe of the executive, and confequently forfeit its virtue and integrity, with refpect to that one territorial government where it refides, it thereby becomes difqualified and unfit to controul the meafures of any one other government: for the judge who is himfelf corrupt, is but little qualified to judge or punifh corruption in others. I therefore conclude that, in order to preferve the virtue and integrity of this controuling deputation, it is indifpenfably neceffary that it fhould not refide within the limits of any one of thefe territorial govern-

R   ments;

ments; thefe being the governments
which it is meant to controul.

On the other hand, it is equally certain,
that this controuling deputation cannot execute in perfon, or affume any perfonal fhare
in the execution of meafures, in any one of
thofe governments where it doth not actually refide; it being impoffible that it
can act perfonally where it is not perfonally prefent. It therefore follows that, by
fituating or placing this controuling deputation at a fufficiently proper diftance from
all thefe feveral territorial governments, it
may be prevented from affuming a perfonal fhare in the immediate execution of
meafures in any one of them. And being
thus, by the fituation of its refidence,
cut off from all opportunity of acting
perfonally, it may likewife be precluded
from acting fecondarily, or ufurping by
proxy any influence, in the immediate execution of thefe governments, if it fhall,
after the manner of the Dutch government at Batavia, be ftrictly prohibited
from exercifing its fuperviling authority
any where without the limits of its own
fixed refidence; and from delegating or
deputing its powers to any perfon or perfons,

fons, its own members or others, who
fhall refide, or may be beyond thefe prefcribed bounds. For though the fyftem
of the Dutch government at Batavia is,
in many refpects, far too rude and unpo-
lifhed; yet is it, in this particular, moft
nicely circumfcribed : that government
being reftrained, in the moft precife manner, from delegating and transferring its
authority ; or from deputing any power
to examine into cafes, of even the moft
dubious nature, within the fubordinates :
but to obviate any inconvenience, that
might otherwife arife from fuch reftraint,
it hath a power to call before it, from the
fubordinates, all perfons or records neceffary to information. For the Dutch were
well aware, that the fupreme government,
if it fhould be permitted to carry its fu-
pervifing authority on any pretext into the
fubordinates, would gain an occafion of
interfering in the execution of thofe meafures which it was intended to controul.
  We muft then perceive, that this controuling deputation being feated at a properly fufficient diftance from all thefe territorial governments, and the exercife of
its powers being exprefsly confined to that

R 2   par-

particular feat of refidence, it will, by fuch
means, be effectually reftrained from interfering, in any fhape, either directly or
indirectly, in the execution of any one of
thofe governments which it is intended to
controul. And we muft farther perceive
that, by virtue of fuch effectual reftraint,
that clear feparation of office, which alone
can prevent the junction or union of the
powers, interefts, and views of this controuling deputation with thofe of the executive, will be completely accomplifhed.
Seeing that, the action of the controuling
power being ftrictly confined within the
limits of its own proper fphere, the executive power muft remain at full liberty
to act diftinctly and freely in the office
affigned to it by the fovereign.

The principal fource of corruption, and
grand ftumbling block of virtue, being
thus removed, the integrity of this controuling deputation may be eftablifhed on
a firm and folid bafis, by fkilfully dividing
the parts which go to compofe it: and,
in particular, by clearly feparating the political and judicial powers : which, if they
fhall be judicioufly divided into two diftinct
departments, mutually independent and
unin-

uninfluenced, will, each of them, act as
an effectual check, and powerful impulse,
on the other: so as to prevent either from
abusing its authority, or neglecting its
duty. Whereas, if the political power
should, at same time, possess the power of
judging, trying and determining, or should
even possess any influence over the judicature, there is danger that it might, on
some occasions, sacrifice its duty to its interest. And this is the very capital error
of the Dutch system at Batavia, inasmuch
as that government, possessing the judicial
power, hath thereby the opportunity of
perverting justice, sometimes to the prejudice of its constituent, and often to the
detriment of its subordinates.

Nor would we be here understood to
signify, by judicial power, a simple court
of judicature, established for the purpose
of deciding litigated cases of property;
the judicial power here meant, must extend
to every thing that respects a due execution
of the jurisdiction and police, in the subordinate governments. Therefore its authority must not be passive, and confined
to such matter as shall come before it by
complaint; but it must be active, assum-

ing

ing cognizance of all public nuiſance,
treſpaſs, or delinquency, that may be
brought before it by information. For,
here, juries may exiſt with great propriety and efficacy, ſeeing that the Company will, on account of her commerce,
keep a number of ſervants at this ſupreme
ſettlement; there will likewiſe be, no
doubt, many free merchants (as they are
termed): and, conſequently, there will
never be wanting a choice of perſons unconnected with, and uninfluenced by the
political government; and therefore fit to
form a grand inqueſt; as well as petit or
ſpecial juries, to decide in either criminal
caſes, or diſputes of property. And this
judicial power muſt farther be endued with
all proper and neceſſary officers; particularly an attorney general: it muſt likewiſe be divided into diſtinct courts; re-
ſembling, as nearly as circumſtances will
admit, or occaſion requires, the courts
of juſtice in the ſovereign country.

Nevertheleſs, we do not preſume to dic-
tate or preſcribe the exact or complete form
of this judicial power: we would only
hint at the main purpoſes of its inſtitution;
a due conſideration of which will readily
                                        ſuggeſt

suggest the particular form, to those whose province it may be to construct it. We shall only observe that, in order to confer a due weight on the judicial power, it is not sufficient that it should be independent, in its corporate capacity; the judges and officers composing it must, in their personal capacity, be placed as far as possible beyond the influence of the political power. The salaries annexed to their offices must be such as will afford dignity, as well as independance: whilst, on the other hand, they shall be debarred, under the severest penalties, from holding, either directly or indirectly, any place, post, emolument, or employment, of any nature, distinct from that of its own proper department. Moreover, the political power should hold no voice in conferring the degrees of this department: that should be vested in the judicial power itself, with reference to the confirmation of the sovereign.

This judicial power may be termed the supreme Court of Judicature, for the whole British dominion in India : to which all the subjects, under the several governments, whether natives or Europeans, may

readily

readily appeal, againft the oppreffion of
their governors, or the perverfion of juftice : and, on which they may fecurely
depend for redrefs ; provided it fhall be
placed above the influence of the political
power. This fupreme court of judicature would likewife be of inexpreffible
utility, as a check on the power, and an
impulfe on the will, of the political
branch.

We may add, that a judicious fubdivi-
fion of the political power, into different
departments, might contribute confiderably to its virtue.

Thefe are the outlines of that meafure,
by which we propofe to preferve this controuling deputation free from corruption :
and we doubt not but, upon this plan,
when meliorated and improved by the fuperior underftanding of others, a controuling power may be conftructed, which
fhall be completely qualified, in point of
virtue and integrity, to faithfully and honourably fuperintend, enforce, and controul the execution of political government in thofe Indian dominions. And
this is, by far, the moft difficult, delicate,
and important part of the undertaking.

For,

For, as to the power and ability, requisite to qualify this deputation for effectually fulfilling the purpose of its institution, that is readily bestowed. The degree of power is altogether in the dispo-
sal of the sovereign. And, its efficacy or
ability depends, principally, upon the
choice of such a situation for the feat of
its residence, as shall enable it to keep up,
at all seasons, a ready and speedy corre-
spondence with the several subordinate governments,

With regard to the choice of situation
proper for the residence of this controuling power; (which is indeed a point of
high importance,) we shall readily conceive, from adverting to its nature and
the purposes of its institution, that this
residence ought to be some convenient sea
port; situated at a considerable distance
from the limits of all these territorial governments; but, at same time, so centrically near to each, that the communication, to and from it, shall, in either mon-
soon, be not only practicable, but certain
and speedy. I shall reserve the farther
explanation of this intended feat of residence, till I come to treat of the military

S   system;

system ; becaufe there are fome properties,
particularly requifite to a proper centre of
military defence : and it is propofed that
the fame power, and confequently the
fame refidence, that fuperintends the
political government, fhould likewife direct the military government and defence,
of this dominion.

But this fupreme controuling power being thus centrically fituated, with refpect
to the feveral fubordinates, as that it fhall
at all times hold a ready and fpeedy cor-
refpondence with each, will be thereby
enabled to effectually fuperintend, enforce,
and controul the execution of political
government in that whole dominion. For,
in the firft place, the ready and fpeedy,
communication with all the fubordinates,
affording to the fupreme power an opportunity of obtaining, from each, the moft
early intelligence of every tranfaction, in-
cident, or occurrence ; as likewife of immediately tranfmitting the orders and inftructions, that may be fuitable to the occafion ; will cut off from the feveral governors of the territorial dominions all
pretext for acting difcretionally. And,
in confequence, that defpotic and arbitrary
power,

power, which hath fubfifted under the
Company's fyftem, will be completely fuppreffed.   And, from adverting to this circumftance, we fhall perceive the importance of a proper choice of fituation, for
this fupreme center of government.

In the fecond place, this ready corref-
pondence with all the fubordinate governments, enabling the fupreme power to
acquire a minute and complete knowledge
of every circumftance, refpecting the ftate
and nature of the general police, in this
whole dominion, will qualify it for originally planning, and for afterwards improving, all fuch defigns and meafures as
can contribute to the inftitution of regularity and good order.   It will likewife
attain an intimate knowledge of the whole
manoeuvre of finance, refpecting the mode
of collecting as well as appropriating the
revenue and taxes : and it will be thereby
enabled to project judicious forms, with
different offices, as mutual checks upon
each other, in that branch : which will
ferve to remedy that incredible extortion,
rapine, and peculation : which, by ruining the farmer of the lands, hath almoft
totally fuppreffed agriculture, and greatly

depo-

depopulated thofe miferable countries; whilft it hath grievoufly defrauded the fovereign of his right. And all thefe planned modes, being approved and confirmed by the fovereign, would be continued in vigorous and perpetual action, by the vicinity of the fupreme political power : and all thefe feveral meafures, being enacted into laws, the ftrict obfervance of them would be effectually enforced by the fame vicinity. And thus, that fupreme power will, not only eftablifh, but perpetually conferve a juft regularity in police, and an exact oeconomy in finance.

In the third place, the fupreme judicial power will, by its neighbourhood to thefe dependent dominions, acquire a juft knowledge of the modes, cuftoms, and difpofitions of the inhabitants; and, by that, it will be enabled to devife the beft forms or offices, together with fkilful rules for adminiftring the jurifdiction, in a manner truly effectual, and at fame time confonant and agreeable to the humour of the fubject. It will likewife be capable of afterwards improving and adding to thefe forms and rules, as future occafion may require, or better information may fuggeft. All which

which forms or offices may, by the approbation of the fovereign, be eftablifhed into ftanding courts; and the rules enacted
into laws. And a punctual obfervance of
all thefe laws enacted, either for the regular adminiftration of juftice, or confer-
vance of the police, will be completely
enforced, by the awe of this fupreme
tribunal: the communication with which,
from all parts of that dependent dominion, being eafy and fpeedy, will afford a
ready accefs and opportunity to all the
fubjects, of prefenting their complaints,
againft any oppreffion of their government, or denial, or perverfion of juftice:
whilft the fame ready communication will
render the trial of all litigated cafes, fpeedy and eafy. A mighty innovation this,
from the former mode of juftice in thofe
dominions; when it was impoffible for even
Europeans to obtain redrefs, in our diftant precife European courts, againft the
moft glaring oppreffion of government:
and the natives were excluded from even
that diftant and deceitful profpect of remedy.

And in order that the courfe of juftice
may be rendered thoroughly complete, it
may

may be enacted, after the manner of the Dutch, that no perfon, who hath held any office of power or truft within the fubordinates, fhall depart immediately from thence for Europe; but fhall be obliged to repair to the fupreme refidence; there to remain for three months; to the end that any perfon or perfons who may, by any means, have been reftrained, during the exiftence of his office, from preferring their complaint againft him, on the fcore of either public or private trefpafs, may there have the free opportunity of profecuting him.

The fupreme political power fhall immediately appoint to all offices, as well political as military, within the fubordinate governments; with reference held to the future approbation, and confirmation, of the fovereign : and it fhall preferve regular minutes of all fuch appointments, orders, and other tranfactions made in its fupreme capacity; which minutes, together with regular and properly vouched accounts of the collection, as well as the appropriation of the revenue, fhall be punctually tranfmitted, by every occafion, to the fovereign. The judicial power

fhall

shall likewise keep an exact register of all trials, causes, and proceedings; more particularly those of the grand inqueft and affizes: this latter to be signed by all the judges and officers of the court, and attefted by the foremen, with a majority of the juries: two copies of which shall be regularly tranfmitted to Britain; one to the fovereign; and the other to the Company; which, as holding a material intereft and share in thefe law proceedings, hath a claim to such participation of knowledge. All which minutes, accounts, and proceedings, being communicated to the fovereign, will enable him to act as an ultimate check on the political government, the finance, and the jurifdiction of that Indian dominion.

Such is the form of this intermediate power, through which I propofe to convey, into the execution of government in thofe diftant Indian dominions, that plenary exertion of the fovereign's reftraining and compelling power, which, alone, can fuffice to prevent tyranny and anarchy. And notwithftanding the materials are, through hurry and want of time, rude, unpolished and coarfely arranged, yet do I flatter my-

felf,

felf, that candour will allow them to be
folidly good, proper, and fully fufficing to
conftruct, at leaft, the groundplot, or
bafis, of a regular political fyftem. Sure
I am, the high propriety, nay the in-
difpenfable neceffity of fuch a meafure, muft immediately ftrike every perfon who employs his own judgment,
however flightly, to confider, firft, the
nature, interefts, and views of the executive government in thofe Indian dominions; as being foreign, deputed,
mutable, and temporary. Second the
timid, paffive, and flavifhly fubmiffive difpofition of the native fubjects. And third,
the diftance of fituation, betwixt the fovereign refidence, and the fcene of government; which, rendering the immediate reftraint and conftraint of the fovereign perfectly impotent, confers on this
foreign executive deputation an unlimited
and arbitrary power, of promoting its own
perfonal views and intereft, by meafures,
which tend to the intolerable oppreffion
of the wretched inhabitants, and the utter
ruin of thofe fubjected countries; as well
as to the mighty detriment of Britain's
deareft intereft, and the blackeft reproach

to

to her reputation. Nor can all this be remedied or prevented, but by fuch a meafure as is here propofed.

And now we fhall take a flight glance at the operation of this meafure, on the jurifdiction, and police, of the fubordinate dominions. And though, for the fake of perfpicuity, we confine the view to Bengal alone, as being the moft eminent part, yet will the effects be equally felt through the whole.

As to the fundamental eftablifhments of Governors, Councils, &c. thefe are fufficiently obvious; as likewife are the proper chambers of revenue : and thefe, with the minutiæ appointments of inferior offices, will be more properly provided and improved, by the better judgment, true information, and future experience of the fupreme controuling power. Here we mean to offer only one or two hints on the mode of jurifdiction and police.

And firft, with regard to the courts of juftice, I fhould propofe that the mayor's court at Culcutta fhould ftill fubfift, as a court of equity for the whole country : and a moft equitable court it is, if properly regulated : for the truth of which affer-

T   tion,

tion, I appeal to all thofe who knew it previous to that alteration of the Company's charter of juftice, which rendered it dependent on, and fubfervient to, the Governor and Council : never was juftice more exactly or more expeditioufly adminiftered, than it was by this court, previous to that alteration. In order therefore to reflore it to its primitive utility, it ought to be reftored to its original ftate. Let the judges or aldermen, who at prefent compofe it, continue fuch : being fervants to the Company, or free merchants, they muft be unconnected with, and uninfluenced by the national government. And, in the cafe of death, or removal, the vacuum to be fupplied by the court itfelf, from amongft the Company's fervants, or free merchants only : and if any alderman fhall, fubfequent to entering on his office, accept of any poft or place under government, let that be an exprefs difqualification and vacation of his office ; which is to be immediately made good, by the choice of another perfon, properly qualified. The newly elected aldermen to be prefented, for acceptance, to the fupreme

court

court of judicature only. And the officers of this court to be chosen by itself.

But as it would be impossible for the mayor's court to dispatch all the business that might be brought before it, there ought likewise to be a court of law; confisting of a chief justice, with three judges; to be appointed by the sovereign. And this court should guide itself, by such laws as may be enacted for the jurisdiction of those countries; otherwise by equity.

Appeals from this court of law, as well as that of equity, to be made immediately to the supreme court of judicature; and from thence to his Majesty in council.

If it is thought proper, there might be another mayor's court, of the same nature, established at Cossimbuzar, in the neighbourhood of the old capital, Maxadavad.

And as to the forms, for the more universal distribution of justice to the natives, these will be adjusted by the supreme supervising power; as before mentioned. We shall only observe, that their courts of Zemindary and Cutchery are, as they stand at present, a grievous nuisance.

But

But the nobleſt inſtitution for protecting the liberty and property of the ſubject, from the extortion and oppreſſion of their foreign government, and of its inferior train of native harpies, who are infinitely more rapacious than the Europeans, would be that of juries, properly conſtructed. Let the grand inqueſt of the country be held at Culcutta, four times in the year: and let the juries, both grand and petit, be expreſly compoſed of Company's ſervants, or free merchants, Europeans, and none others: the judges of law, or at leaſt two of them, to ſit on the aſſizes: the ſheriff to be choſen annually, from amongſt the Company's ſervants.

The powers of this grand inqueſt, if adapted to the ſituation of things, muſt be enlarged beyond theſe of our juries in Britain; where there are judicial and political aids, that muſt be wanting in thoſe countries: for inſtance, the enquiry muſt not be confined to place, but muſt extend every where through the country : it muſt likewiſe have authority to bring before it all manner of nuiſance or treſpaſs committed againſt the liberty or property of the ſubject, natives as well as Europeans.

And

And the judges should have no power to
reject or poftpone the bills, found by the
grand jury : but should bring them on to
decifion, in turn, as prefented. Moreover,
as the extent of enquiry may render it impoffible for the more diftant defendant to
appear with his evidences, during the fitting of that affize to which the bill hath
been prefented againft him ; let fummons
be iffued, upon the bill's being prefented,
for fuch diftant defendant to appear at next
affizes ; or let fome other method be found,
either by means of the grand jury's meet-
ing a fufficient time before the commencement of trials, or by fome extraordinary power vefted in the judges or fheriff
to produce fuch diftant defendant with his
evidences in due time. And as this fame
extent of enquiry may, on the other hand,
produce inconvenience to the fubject, by
affording occafion to litigious perfons of
diftreffing others, by bringing them from a
great diftance to thefe affizes, on frivolous
or ill grounded complaints, it may be ordered that, where the caufe fhall appear to
the court truly litigious, the plaintiff fhall
be bound over to ftand fuit at law, for da-
mages to the defendant : and, one or two
examples,

examples, of this nature, will prove a barr to frivolous litigation.

And leaft the judges fhould, by any means, be influenced to act that part which the Company's governor and council commonly act, when they abfurdly prefide at thefe affizes, as his Majefty's judges in their own caufe; namely, to difmifs the Court, fo foon as the grand jury fhall find a bill that may be difagreeable to them; it may be ordered that neither the judges, nor any officer of the Court, fhall have power to adjourn the affizes, until all the trials fhall be decided; or, otherwife, by the confent of a majority in both juries.

The principal check however upon the conduct of thefe affizes, would be that of obliging the Court to keep exact regifters, of all trials, and proceedings; figned and attefted, as before mentioned. And if any part of either jury fhall except to the authenticity of fuch regifter, which fhall be publickly expofed in the Court, then, fuch diffenting part fhall have a right to proteft, and affign its reafons. Three copies of which regifter, with proteft, (if any,) fhall be difpatched, by the earlieft occafion, after each affize. One copy to the

the fupreme Court of Judicature, which will, thereby, have the earlieft notice of any abufe; and, with the concurrence of the fupreme political power, fhall have the opportunity of immediately correcting it. A fecond copy fhall be tranfmitted to the fovereign; who will act as an ulterior check on the fupreme controuling power. And a third copy to the Company for the reafons before fpecified.

But, as this fingle inqueft at Calcutta cannot poffibly carry juftice to the extremes of that extenfive country, circulating affizes may be held, at leaft once, or if poffible twice a year, at Muxadavad as the center, and at Patnah as the northern extreme; two judges to go this northern circuit: and the other two judges to go on an eaftern circuit, at Dacca. And, as there may not be a fufficient number of Company's fervants, properly qualified, to form complete juries at thefe northern and eaftern affizes: I would propofe that, to make up any fuch deficiency, natives fhould be mixed with the Europeans. Which mixture, if it fhall be artfully tempered, in the following manner, would produce all the efficacy of entirely

tirely European juries; and, at fame time, none of the bad effects, that might be apprehended, from an attempt to confer freedom and impartiality on juries entirely native.

Let, at leaft, one half of both the grand and petit juries be Europeans; and the remaining part natives: and if it fhould happen, that there cannot be collected, at the affize factory, and from the neighbouring inferior factories, fo many Company's fervants as fhall make up half the ufual number of jurymen; then, let the whole number be diminifhed, to the fufficing half of Europeans. Let the unanimity of verdict, in fuch mixt juries, be difpenfed with; and let the majority of voices, in either jury, find the bill or verdict; as is the cuftom in Scotland. And let an additional provifion be made to the oath of the juryman, purporting that he fhall not, on any account, difclofe the opinion given by any individual, in the jury room.

By this artful mixture, and thefe precautions, the native jurymen would be liberated from that flavifh dread, of future revenge from their own countrymen employed

ployed under government; feeing it would
be impoſſible, for theſe native officers of
government, to diſcover the particular opinion of each individual; which, if the
juries were entirely native, they would
infallibly do, to the utter ruin of the poor
native jurymen. So that the native Jurymen, acting thus with freedom, under the
cloke and protection of the Europeans,
would anſwer all the effectual purpoſes of
Europeans. Whilſt, being ſenſible that
they owed their freedom and impartiality,
together with all the other benefits ariſing
from juries, to their connection with the
Europeans; this freedom conferred on
them in the jury room, would not in the
leaſt diminiſh their awe and deference to
government. The proceedings at theſe
circuit aſſizes to be regiſtered and tranſ-
mitted in like manner as at Calcutta.

'Theſe juries would prove the Magna
Charta, the palladium, and true ſecurity
of Indian liberty and property, againſt the
deſpotiſm and extortion of their foreign
government. And it evidently appears,
that the virtue of theſe juries, (as being,
at one and the ſame time, truly effectual
to the ſubject, and perfectly ſafe to the

U   ſove-

sovereign,) entirely depends upon the circumstance, of completely excluding the
Company and her servants, from the small-
est participation in the executive powers
of government. But the efficacy of these
juries, and of other inferior institutions
made through the supreme controuling
power, being once felt and known, would
speedily induce the natives to purchase
perpetual property in lands ; seeing they
would perceive themselves thoroughly secured in the produce of those lands. And
this, being divulged abroad, would draw
the inhabitants of the neighbouring countries to the standard of Britain ; together
with their wealth, and industry. By
which means the British dominion in India, which, at present is, through oppression and consequent famine, in a great
measure deserted and depopulated, would
again be completely peopled and cultivated:
arts, manufactures, and commerce would
soon be restored to their former state ; nay,
they would be extended to a degree far
superior: and these countries would, of
course, be enabled to richly repay Britain
for the blessings conferred by her, of per-

fect

fect fecurity in liberty and property; blef-
fings, never before known in India.

And all this may be effected by means
of that intermediate fupreme controuling
power: which would, not only create,
but preferve, the full and vigorous efficacy
of all thefe inftitutions, in the fubordinate
dominions. Whereas, if it was even poffible, (though indeed it is morally impoffible,) to inftitute, by any temporary
means, all thefe powers, forms, rules,
and regulations in thofe dominions, yet
is it evidently certain that, fo foon as thefe
temporary means were withdrawn, the
virtue and efficacy of all thefe inftitutions
would immediately vanifh, and be fuppreffed by the power of the executive government; which, from the nature of
things, muft unavoidably be, either defpotic over the native fubjects, or cannot
exift at all.

But this fame controuling power, as it
would, on the one hand, by its fixed refidence in the immediate neighbourhood,
perpetually preferve the action and motion
of all thefe inftitutions, like to a power
ever prefent to wind up the fprings of the
machine; and, fo, would check all the

bad

bad effects of that naturally neceſſary deſpotiſm in executive government : ſo would
it, on the other hand, effectually ſupport
the power and authority of that executive
government; and prevent its being en-
croached on, by an over exertion of the
privileges conferred on the ſubject. For,
on this ſide too, there is a danger; which
will be readily comprehended, by thoſe
who conſider the nature of government;
and, at ſame time, the diſpoſition of human nature. But all danger, of prepon-
derating either ſcale, would be prevented,
by the vicinity of the controuling power :
which, holding the balance in its hands,
and nicely diminiſhing from one, or
adding to the other ſcale, would ever preſerve a juſt equilibrium, betwixt the liberty of the ſubject, and the power of
government.

Nor would the inſtitution of new regulations be the only means, in the hands
of the controuling power, of preventing
the dangerous over exertion of privilege ;
it would likewiſe poſſeſs the inſtantaneous
power of ſeizing, or otherwiſe of ordering
to its own reſidence, all ſuch perſons as
ſhould prove over troubleſome, or dangerous

to

to the due authority of executive government. For, though it would be extremely
abfurd to truft a power of this nature, immediately in the hands of executive government; which would, infallibly, em-
ploy it to its own worft purpofes : yet
might fuch power be fafely trufted to this
controuling government; which could not
have the fame motives to abufe it.

Neverthelefs, we do not mean that this,
and all thefe other powers, fhould be un-
limitedly confided to this controuling deputation : we ftill preferve a check over
it, in the national government. And a
moft effectual check too ; by means of the
beforementioned copies of regifters, immediately tranfmitted to Britain, from the
fubordinates; as likewife by its own minutes, accounts, and regifters.

So that here would be a regular grada-
tion of effectual political checks. The
privilege of juries, and other inftitutions
in the fubordinate dominions, being preferved in vigorous action, by the influence
of the intermediate controuling power,
would prove an effectual check on the defpotifm or extortion of executive government; and would thus completely fecure
the

the liberty and property of the fubject.
And the fame influence of the controuling
power would fufficiently check the luxu-
riancy of privilege ; and fupport the power
of government ; thus preferving an exact
poife betwixt both. Whilft the fovereign,
at a diftance, could deliberately and effectually watch the hand that trimmed the
fcales.

And thus the inftitution of this intermediate controuling and impelling power,
would completely remove every obftruction arifing from the diftance of fituation ;
it would ferve as an intermediate link of
the political chain : or, as a bridge of
communication, joining this dependent
Indian dominion to the fovereign country. But, all obftruction arifing from the
diftance of fituation being thus removed,
what difficulty can the national government of Britain find, in adminiftring the
political government of that Indian dominion ? Upon this plan, that tafk appears
to me more facil, lefs pregnant with difficulty, charge, or care, than it is to govern
any one, the moft pretty, of our foreign
Colonies : nay it appears equally eafy, as
it is to govern the neighbouring Ifle of
Man :

Man : feeing that the oppofition of the
fubjects, to the authority of government
in this Indian dominion, though they be fo
infinitely more numerous, is not greater
than is the oppofition of the few fubjects in Man. The only difficulty, that
could exift to national government, was
that of duly tempering, or abating, the
power of the deputed executive government : and it appears, that this may be
completely effected by means of this
intermediate controuling power; which,
in the hands of the fovereign, would act
upon the government of this Indian dominion as the pegs or keys upon the ftrings of
a mufical inftrument; of which one
being gently ftrained, and another properly relaxed, would create, and perpetually
preferve, a perfect harmony, or concord,
in this political fyftem.

A

ESTABLISHING A REGULAR SYSTEM

OF

MILITARY GOVERNMENT,

AND OF

SECURE DEFENCE,

IN

INDIA.

THE Company's fyftem of military
government and defence in India is,
at leaft, equally defective, faulty, and abfurd ; and, therefore, doth equally demand
reformation, as doth her political fyftem.
For the fame caufe that renders the power
of the Company's feveral deputed governors perfectly arbitrary and difcretional,
in civil matters ; namely, the Directors
having preferved to themfelves the charge
of immediately directing and fuperintending thofe governments ; confers, upon
thefe deputed governors, a like arbitrary
and difcretional power, in military matters. And furely it is impoffible to conceive any thing more ridiculoufly extravagant

vagant, than is this military fyftem of the
Company; which affords to each governor, of four different capital fettlements,
the abfolute, independent, and difcretional power, of applying the military force
of his own government; and likewife of
directing the meafures of defence : whilft,
each, of thefe four governors, holds a particular intereft of his own ; which is, not
only diftinct from, but oppofite to that of
all the others.

Can it be fuppofed that four men, thus
oppofite in their perfonal views and interefts, and thus independent of each other,
fhould heartily concur in general meafures;
or fhould cordially unite in a fyftem of
common defence ? Common fenfe informs
us that they will not; and experience con-
vinces us that they do not. For it hath
been known that one, of thefe fettlements,
hath furnifhed arms and ammunition;
and hath otherwife befriended a power,
at open war with one of the others. And,
in the cafe of any one of thefe fettlements being attacked, the others are extremely backward in fupporting it; becaufe each, of the four governors, giving
the preference to his own particular

charge,

charge, in which his own perfonal intereft is more immediately concerned, confiders all communication of his force, to any of the other fettlements, as a diminution of his own fecurity, and even of his importance. So that, upon fuch terms, the union betwixt thefe four diftinct, and mutually independent, governments, can fcarcely be termed federal.

Moreover, each of thefe four governors poffeffes, within the limits of his own government, the difcretionary power of making war and peace. And, fo, hath the opportunity, whenever it fhall fuit the purpofe of his own perfonal intereft, to pick a quarrel, and engage his government in war, with fome one of the neighbouring native ftates. Nor is this an imaginary evil ; or a fimple fuppofition of what may poffibly happen ; it is a real cafe ; an abufe that hath actually exifted. For we can produce feveral inftances where thefe governors, more particularly on the coaft of Cormondel, have commenced, and induftrioufly protracted, wars with the neighbouring ftates, exprefsly for the purpofe of plunder and peculation,

And,

And, from this difcretionary power of peace and war lodged in the hands of thefe feveral governors, and the confequent abufe thereof, flow the following evils to the fovereign. Firft, the governor, thus warring, exhaufts and confumes the treafure of his conftituent; to the end that he and his affociates, may gain occafion to pocket a part. Second, by thefe offenfive wars, he waftes and deftroys that force, which was intended by the fovereign for defence: and, thereby, expofes his own charge, naked and defencelefs, to the attack of other enemies. And third, by thefe wanton unneceffary and unjuft wars, he provokes the hatred and jealoufy of all the neighbouring ftates; and, thus, converts into enemies, thofe native powers, who would, otherwife, be amicable and friendly to the fovereign.

To correct thefe, and many other abufes of a like nature, which flow from this abfurd military fyftem of the Company, it is evidently and indifpenfably neceffary, that there fhould be inftituted, one fupreme head of military government. Which, being vefted with the fupreme power of making peace and war in India,

fhall

shall restrain these several territorial governors, from engaging in unnecessary wars with their neighbours. And which, possessing the supreme direction of the common force, shall, in the case of particular or general danger, apply that force to the most proper and necessary purposes.

Now it is naturally proper, that the same intermediate supreme power, which superintends the political government, should likewise supremely superintend the military government, and defence, of those Indian dominions. And, for this latter purpose, the choice of a proper situation, for the residence of that supreme power, becomes likewise a point of most essential consequence. For it is evident, on the one hand, that this military superintending power ought not to exist in any one of these territorial governments; nay it ought not to reside in the immediate neighbourhood of any one rich native state; because, in either of these two situations, it is liable to be tempted, by views of avarice or ambition, to apply the general force, to its own personal purposes; and, if so, the cure would be worse than the disease: and, on the other hand, it is

no

no lefs evident, (from the reafons affigned
on the fimilar head in the political fyftem)
that this fupreme military power ought to
be fituated fo centrically near, to all the
feveral territorial governments, as that it
may, at all times and feafons, be capable
of keeping up a ready and fpeedy corre-
fpondence with each.

The diftant and unconnected fituation,
of thefe four capital governments, is likewife a mighty obftruction to a fecure fyftem of defence. For, the wind, blowing in thofe feas for fix months from one
quarter of the compafs, and for the other
fix months from the oppofite quarter, doth,
alternately, cut off in a great meafure all
naval communication betwixt thefe four
governments. For inftance, during the
violence of the fouth weft monfoon, that
is, from the middle of April till the middle of July, it is almoft impracticable for
fhips to pafs from Bengal to Madrafs : and,
during the three more moderate months
of that monfoon, this paffage is difficult
and tedious. And during the north eaft
monfoon, the paffage is much the fame
from Madrafs to Bengal. But the communication betwixt Bombay, and thefe

two

two fettlements, is ftill more obftructed.
For Bombay, being fituated in lat. 19 deg.
north, on the weft fide of the peninfula
of India, it is almoft impoffible, from the
latter end of November till the middle of
February, for fhips from Bombay, bound
for the Bay of Bengal, to round the ifland
of Ceyloan: and, for the other three
months of the north eaft monfoon, they
are obliged, in order to weather Ceyloan,
to ftand over to the eaftward almoft as far
as Atchen head, and back again to the
ifland; a run of about 20 degrees. From
the end of April till Auguft, it is almoft
impracticable for fhips from the Bay and
bound for Bombay, to round Ceyloan;
and in the other three months of the fouth
weft monfoon, that paffage is difficult and
tedious. And, even in the fair paffage,
the run betwixt Bengal and Bombay is
feldom made in lefs than a month. Moreover, during the force of the fouth weft
monfoon on the weft fide of the peninfula, that is, from the middle of May till
the middle of Auguft, it is extremely dangerous for fhips to attempt running in for
Bombay: the weather being then fo extremely thick, that fometimes a folar obfervation

fervation cannot be obtained for feveral days together : and if a fhip fhould, in fuch circumftances, run in for the land, which in fuch weather is not diftinguifh-able at three leagues diftance, and fhould mifs the opening of the harbour, which is but fmall, it is more than probable that fhe would not be able to clear the fhore, with the wind blowing fiercely right on, and rolling before it a heavy fea. As to Bencolen, circumftances are nearly the fame with it, as betwixt Bengal and Ma-drafs.

Now it is evident, that this obftructed naval communication, betwixt the four chief governments muft, in many refpects, greatly weaken the common defence : and muft greatly augment, to the fove-reign, the charge, in both men and mo-ney, of maintaining and defending thofe dominions and poffeffions. Seeing it muft neceffitate him to keep up, in each of thofe governments, a force fufficient to defend it againft the whole united ftrength of an offenfive enemy, without trufting to any aid from the others : becaufe, other-wife, he runs the rifk of lofing them all

fingly,

fingly, to a force that can overpower but one of them.

But all the danger, inconveniences, and extraordinary expence, arifing from this obftructed naval communication, may be obviated and removed, by eftablifhing one fupreme center of military defence; fo fituated, with refpect to the feveral parts of thofe truly valuable territorial dominions, as that the communication betwixt it and them fhall, in either monfoon, be not only practicable but fpeedy and eafy. For it is evident that, in fuch a fituation, this fupreme center of defence could, at all times, receive fpeedy notice of any impending danger, or actual attack; and that, upon fuch notice, it could immediately tranfport its own garrifon, by fea; as well as collect aid from the other fettlements. So that the garrifon of this fupreme center of defence would act as an army of obfervation; ever ready to pour in, at any quarter, on the back of an aggreffive enemy. And, of courfe, fuch a center of defence muft connect, and unite, the ftrength of all the feveral parts of Britifh dominion in India.

Now

Now it appears that, the fituation of refidence, becomes a circumftance, highly effential to the efficacy of each purpofe, propofed from this fupreme intermediate power. And it farther appears that one, and the fame, fituation is required, for all thefe feveral purpofes : feeing that, from a convenient naval port, fituated at a proper diftance from the limits of all the territorial governments; and, at fame time, fo centrically near to each, that the communication with all the feveral parts of dominion will be fpeedy and eafy; this fupreme power would, in the firft place, completely and effeꝗtually, faithfully and honourably fuperintend, enforce, and controul the meafures of political government, as well as the conduꝗt of military government : and, in the fecond place, it would unite and conneꝗt the general ftrength of thofe dominions, and completely fecure the defence of the whole.

But, of the feveral fettlements poffeffed by the Company in India, Bengal and Madrafs are evidently difqualified for this feat of refidence; not only becaufe the communication betwixt them and the other fettlements is, at certain feafons, altogether cut

Y   off;

off; but becaufe they are, themfelves, territorial governments; and therein, the very object to be controuled. Bencolen is, in every
refpect, out of the queftion. And, there
then remains only Bombay; which is fo
far poffeffed of the properties requifite to
this refidence, in that it is, at prefent, not
greatly embarked in territorial dominion;
and is, likewife, a fea port. But in refpect of communication, with the truly
valuable poffeffions of Britain in India,
Bombay is altogether unfit to be either the
refidence of the fupreme controuling power, or yet the center of defence; as muft
appear from the preceding defcription;
which was more particularly enlarged,
for the exprefs purpofe of evincing this.
Far from being a proper center of defence, all the force that is lodged at Bombay becomes detached, and completely
loft to the defence of Britain's truly valuable poffeffions; at leaft on any fudden e-
mergency. Indeed Bombay is, in every
thing, refpecting either dominion or commerce, a dead load, and ufelefs fettlement;
faving it be for the fole purpofe of a naval
port, or a place for refitting our fquadrons.

But

But the choice of Bombay for a naval port, is the moſt dangerous and fatal error, in the whole abſurd ſyſtem of the Company's defence: ſeeing that, by this abſurd choice, Britain loſes the uſe of her naval force; which is her capital ſtrength of defence, againſt the attack of France, her only dangerous enemy in India—As will appear—It is impoſſible that ſhips, the beſt fitted from Europe, can ſubſiſt, in thoſe ſeas, for two years, without a thorough repair: and more particularly in time of war; when action hath happened, and is again expected. And this thorough repair they cannot obtain but in a naval port, properly filled with docks, or careening platforms. Bombay is the only naval port, thus fitted by Britain, in India; conſequently the ſquadron of Britain muſt retire, at leaſt every ſecond year, to Bombay, for repair. But the Britiſh ſquadron being once retired to Bombay, (as is common, in October;) which is ſituated in lat. 19 degrees north, on the weſt ſide of the peninſula; it is as effectually excluded, for five months, from the bay of Bengal, and more particularly from Bengal itſelf, as if it was ſtill in Europe. And,

during

during thefe five months, the enemy may
either fcour that Bay with fingle cruizers,
or fhe may tranfport, and, without oppofition, land a force in Bengal; and thefe
faid five months are the very fitteft in the
whole year for land operations. This muft
be thoroughly underftood by all thofe who
are acquainted with the navigation of thofe
feas: and could be here readily demonftrated; was it not that, by publickly
pointing out our own weaknefs, we fhould
point out to the enemy her ftrength.
It is moft certain that, if France underftands her own advantage, (and it is to be
apprehended fhe is but too well acquainted
with it) fhe may either wafte and confume
the Britifh fquadron, through preventing its
repair; or otherwife fhe may effect every
purpofe, againft Bengal, nay againft Madrafs, with as great fecurity, as if there
was no Britifh fquadron in India: ever fo
long as Britain fhall continue her only naval port at Bombay.   Nor is there any alternative.   For as to that ridiculous notion, of carrying a fquadron of large fhips
up the river of Bengal to repair, no com-
mander in his fenfes would, in the time of
war, when he expected to be equally
matched

matched by the enemy, fo foon as the fea-
fon arrived, incur the rifk of lofing fome
of his fhips, in the paffage up and down
that incredibly dangerous river; and ftill
lefs would he fubject himfelf to the certainty of lofing half his hands, by that
putrid unhealthy air at Culpee, or Ingelee.
Neither would he be mad enough, in the
while of a hot war, to ufe that dangerous
expedient, of half repairing at Trinca-
malay; where he is liable to be furprized
by an enemy, in the act of repairing. In
fine, fo long as Bombay continues to be
our only naval port, our commanders
muft, of neceffity, either wafte and lofe
their fquadron; or elfe they muft retire to
Bombay, at the leaft, once in two years;
and, thereby leave the feas, with all our
valuable poffeffions in the Bay of Bengal,
freely expofed to the attack of an enemy,
for five months.

It therefore follows that, if Britain
means to avail herfelf of her naval force,
which is the principal defence of her dominion and commerce in India, fhe muft
eftablifh a proper naval port, on the eaft
fide of the peninfula; becaufe, on that
fide lay all her truly valuable poffeffions,
and

and commerce. And that port, which I mean to propofe, is in every refpect completely qualified for this purpofe : though I cannot, in this publication, fpecify the place; left the enemy fhould anticipate, and take the advantage of our fhameful neglect.

I am fenfible it will be immediately exclaimed that we have already too many poffeffions in India ; and that this is no time to increafe our fettlements there ; and thereby to increafe the drain of our native ftrength, as well as the expence of treafure.

But, to this, I anfwer, that this new eftablifhment would not encreafe the number of our capital fettlements in India : on the contrary, it would diminifh it, from four to three : for it would fupprefs, in the firft place, Bombay ; which is in every refpect a truly ufelefs fettlement; and would therefore be exchanged for this new fettlement; which would ferve to connect the whole ftrength of this dominion ; as well as to promote a variety of other very important purpofes. In the fecond place, Bencolen would be reduced to the degree of a fubordinate, immediately under the

direction

direction of the refident at this new fettlement; and completely fecure under its
protection. .

As to the drain of native ftrength, this
eftablifhment would, inftead of adding,
confiderably decreafe it: for the garrifon,
together with the artillery, &c. of Bombay,
would be tranfported thither; as likewife
would the better part of the garrifon at
Bencolen: and thefe two garrifons, being
placed there, would form an army of obfervation, for all our valuable poffeffions,
as hath been defcribed; confequently the
territorial governments would not demand
that degree of force, which is requifite at
prefent, when each ftands on its own
bottom.

And with regard to the expence of
treafure, I fhall only obferve that, it is
moft unaccountably abfurd in Britain to
fend out to India, a fquadron of 17 fhips
of the line, befides frigates, (as fhe did in
laft war,) for the protection of her dominion and commerce in that country; which
fquadrons become evidently unprofitable
to that purpofe, through the circumftance
of wanting a properly fituated naval port;
when lefs than a fingle year's charge, of
fuch

such squadron, would suffice to completely fit up a naval port, so situated as that,
from thence, her naval force would completely effect its intended purpose. For I
affirm, that the port which I propose would
be completely fitted up, in every respect,
as a naval port, for less expence than one
year's charge of such squadron; seeing
that I do not propose docks, but platforms
for careening, as at Batavia; and these are
prepared, in infinitely less time, and at
much less charge than docks; whilst they
are far more convenient and expeditious
for repairing large ships, than these docks
at Bombay. And, as to the fortification
immediately requisite, it would be but little expensive, and would demand but little time to rear it: because it would be
perfectly accessible to the ships; and so,
whilst it protected them, would be protected by them.

Moreover no part of the treasure, expended on originally fitting this naval port,
would come immediately out of Britain's
proper treasury; for the whole would be
defrayed by the dependent dominion in
India. And this new establishment would,
in a very little time, not only support its

own

own charge, but would richly reimburfe Britain for her original coft. Seeing it would, in the firft place, as a colony or fettlement, yield her immediate treafure, together with fundry commodities peculiar to itfelf; and, in a little time, it would, under proper conduct, produce rich manufactures. In the fecond place, it would, as an Emporium, (for which purpofe it is perfectly adapted by its fituation,) greatly improve the commerce of Britain in India : and as a centrical magazine or warehoufe, for the commodities of China as well as India, it would reduce the term of the Company's voyages to one year; and, thereby, reducing the expence of her carriage nearly one third, it would enable her to fell cheaper; and confequently advance her commerce in Europe. Likewife the Company's fhips rendezvoufing and departing from this port for Europe, under proper convoy, this would fecure her trade from that imminent danger to which it is expofed, from her fhips rendezvoufing fingly, at that button of an ifland, St. Helena : a circumftance that may, in the very firft year of a French war, completely ruin this Company; as

Z   that

that enemy is now perfectly acquainted
with her route. Now Bombay is perfectly
ufelefs to all thefe, and indeed to every
other purpofe; as can be readily demonftrated : and the whole benefit derived from
it, as a colony or fettlement, in the year, doth
not fuffice to defray one month's expence.

But this new eftablifhment, being once
fitted up as a naval port, from whence the
fquadrons of Britain can, in either monfoon, command all her valuable poffeffions;
this fame eftablifhment would, at fame
time, completely fuit for the refidence of
that fupreme intermediately fuperintending
power. For this port is fituated, at fuch
a diftance from all the territorial governments, as would fuffice to effectually prevent the controuling power, from interfering in the immediate execution of government. And, having faid that it is
perfectly well fituated for a naval port, it
follows that the communication, betwixt
it and all the parts of the Britifh dominion
in India, muft be fpeedy and eafy, in
either monfoon : and confequently that,
from this refidence, this fupreme power can
effectually fuperin tend, enforce, and controul the meafures of political, as well

as

as of military, government, in this whole
dominion. And, being the center of
naval defence, it muſt be the only proper center of land defence : feeing the
ſquadron will be ever at hand, to tranſ-
port its land force, to any part of this
dominion, that may be in danger.

And thus have I accompliſhed that
which I propoſed : having planned the deſign
of an intermediate power which, in ſuch
a ſituation as hath been deſcribed, would
eſtabliſh a completely regular ſyſtem of government, civil as well as military, in
the whole preſent or future dominion of
Britain in India : nay which would, in
the hands of national government, render the taſk of governing this Indian dominion, as facil and eaſy, as it is to govern the ſmall Iſle of Man. And, the
feat of its reſidence being at ſame time
the center of naval and land defence, it
would completely connect the, otherwiſe,
divided ſtrength of the ſeveral governments : and would eſtabliſh the general
defence, upon a footing ſo ſecure, that no
enemy, either European or native, would
dare to attack Britiſh dominion in India.
It likewiſe appears that the drain of native

ſtrength,

ftrength, requifite to maintain this whole
dominion, would but little exceed that
which Britain expends on maintaining the
two barren fortreffes, of Gibraltar and
St. Philips's. Whilft no part of the pecuniary charge, of either eftablifhing or
afterwards fupporting this fyftem of government, nor yet of the land and even
naval defence, would come out of the
treafury of Britain ; but would all be
defrayed by the dependent dominion.

I have farther demonftrated the moral
impoffibility of governing and maintaining
this Indian dominion, by means of the
Company ; upon any other terms, than
thefe, of conftituting her fovereign at home
as well as abroad ; and of conferring, upon her Directors, the fovereign execution
of government in Britain, as well as in
that dependent dominion.

And I have endeavoured to rouze and
awake the nation, to fome fenfe of, and regard to, the intereft fhe holds in this Indian dominion ; by a flight defcriptive
fketch of the nature, and degree, of benefit received by her from it, for fome years
paft. And, as the fenfation received from
fact and experience makes ever a ftronger
impref-

impreffion on the mind, than that which
is conveyed by fpeculative argument, I fhall
here again apply to the experience of the
public, on this topic; which cannot be
too much inculcated, nor prefented in too
many different points of view; at this
truly critical juncture, when nothing lefs
than the moft fpeedy application, of the
moft vigorous meafures, can prevent the
total lofs, of this moft important object to
Britain; either through the final ruin of
the countries themfelves; or, otherwife,
by the affault of enemies.

Britain feels a general failure of credit,
not only in the Eaft India Company, but
in individuals: and this failure of credit
fhe can afcribe to no other caufe, than to
fome extraordinary defect of numerical
circulation, or a deficiency of numerical
fpecie, fufficient to fupport the wonted
credit of paper. How happens this want
of numerical fpecie to be fo feverely felt,
all of a fudden; or from whence fhould
fuch defect arife? Affuredly from a decreafe of her wonted influx of numerical
fpecie; whilft her drain of that fpecie
continues to be at leaft the fame as formerly. But what channel or fource, of
Britain's

Britain's influx, hath been dried up so sud-
denly, as to create this surprizing failure
of numerical circulation ? We have shown
it to originate in Indian dominion ; which
being, through misgovernment, reduced
to a ruinous state, the consequent wonder-
ful decrease of revenue, hath obliged the
Company, to absorb and dry up that channel of Indian private fortunes ; which, till
within these two years, used to convey into
Britain, by foreign Company's bills, &c.
at least 700,000 l. *per annum*, in numerical specie, or what is equivalent. And as
Britain hath, during the two years that
this channel was dried up, been continuing
that drain, which she could barely support, when aided by that private fortune
influx, it is plain that, within these two
years, she must have diminished the standing stock of her numerical circulation,
at least, 1,400,000 l. And one year, more
of only an equally decreased degree of
influx, will diminish her circulating stock
2,100,000 l. and so on. But a total deprivation of the influx received, for some
years past, from Indian dominion, will,
annually, double the diminution of circulating stock.

And,

And, from this view, the nation may draw the following juft inferences : firft, the mighty value and importance, of this Indian dominion, to Britain ; in point of financial aid ; as well as in other weighty refpects. Second, the mighty alteration of circumftances, in thefe Indian coun-tries, fince the time they became fubjected to the dominion of the Company ; as alfo, the prefent ruinous ftate of that domi-nion. And from thefe two inferences fhe may deduce, that conclufion which hath been juft mentioned, that nothing lefs than the moft fpeedy application of the moft vigorous and effectual meafures, can pof-fibly fave thofe countries from final ruin ; and Britain from confequent bankruptcy, poverty, lofs of credit, of commerce, na-vigation, naval power, &c.

I have, in this hafty production, fketch-ed out the nature of the neceffary meafures; but the application of thefe meafures de-pends entirely upon the nation's exerting her own attention. I am far from mean-ing to work upon the paffions, I apply on-ly to the reafon and underftanding of men ; for had not refpect to decorum, and to the dignity of government, reftrained me, I might,

might, on this fubject, have thrown out many things, that muft have excited dif-content and indignation. Neverthelefs the importance and urgency of the cafe obli-ges me to add, (and, without this, all I have faid can avail nothing,) that unlefs the nation fhall exert herfelf moft vigoroufly in this her own deareft concern, fhe muft not look for any fuch effectual meafures, as will fuffice to prevent thefe difafters.

For the nation muft confider, that her prefent adminiftration confifts of the very men who tranfacted, and (by their truly reverberating eccho) confirmed, to the Company, the fecond * grant of the De-wanny : knowing that this Dewanny was nothing other than the fovereignty of a

---

* .We muft make a wide difference betwixt the firft and fecond grants of this Dewanny, (as it is termed.) The firft grant was made for only two years, at a time when the then miniftry were in a great meafure unac-quainted with the nature of the thing which they granted : having been deceived by bafe art : nor did this miniftry, in the courfe of their adminiftration, exert any manner of minifterial influence over the Directors. But far different were the lights, as well as the conduct of that miniftry which, on the expiration of the firft two years, renewed that grant for the long term of five years.

mighty

mighty dominion, dependent upon the Crown, and Nation, of Britain: and, consequently that, by subjecting the numerous inhabitants of those countries to the dominion of a few merchants, incapable of administring any sort of government, they were configning over to tyranny and anarchy, intolerable oppreffion and ruin, many millions of men, who were, to all intents. and purposes, subjects of Britain. And they are the men who, during the four years that elapsed since that grant, have furnished the force to support this tyranny and anarchy: and, in spite of ⸺⸺⸺ ⸺⸺⸺⸺⸺⸺⸺enacting a farce, wherein the Directors were compelled to perform the same part in Europe, that the native Nabobs have exhibited in India. It cannot, therefore, be expected that they will, willingly, change their plan of conduct: seeing that, besides their former motives, they have the additional one of obstinacy; or shame of standing self-condemned, for past mismanagement, should they now alter their measures. It is rather to be supposed that they will continue the cloke of the Company; together with the Directorial farce: and that, to support

the

the broken credit of the Company, (broken by collufive management,) they will, through eccho, grant her a power, to force her paper upon the public, for its money. As also that, under the pretext of honouring the nation with fome fhare in the charge of this fovereignty, (under the Company, but no fhare in the profits,) they will gradually thruft her fhoulders under that whole load, which, as the Company muft manage it, will foon become intolerable. And, by the aid of thefe frefh reinforcements, they will juggle it and bungle it, and bungle it and juggle it on, for one, or poffibly two, years longer : and then Nation and Company will both tumble together, into the pit of bankruptcy, perdition, and defpair.

But fhall the nation, with eyes open, fuffer the pilot to crowd ftemlings on the rocks, which have already grazed the fhip's bottom ? No, we muft about fhip, and call another hand to the helm. Matters, it is to be hoped, are not yet paft remedy ; the channel is obvious ; if the nation will but put to her hand. His Majefty can have no real intereft but what is common with that of his people : and, how-

however the views of the Crown may, in some cases, differ a little from these of the people; in this particular case they muft both exactly concur. He will, here, hearken to the voice of his people: and a little popular heat will force into administration something of that patriotic ambition, fire, spirit, and enterprize, which alone can save this nation from dreadful impending misfortunes.

But if the nation, sunk in the bed of slavish sloth, inebriated with the transforming Circean cap, enervated and emasculated by the lewd embraces of sensual pleasure, shall slight and disregard her own dearest concerns : like the prodigal debauchee, who chides from him the faithful friend that attempts recalling him to sober reflection; and implicitly confides in the management of a steward, who hath already wasted the better part of his fair patrimony : then let the nation, some two or three years hence, recollect, that she was advised of her danger, by a hasty production, issued about the middle of January, 1773 : though not thought of, until that most disinterested of all possible ministers had, by way of remedying all evils,

disdifpatched *his Secret Committee* to the In-. dia Houfe : there to infpect the Company's. private œconomy : a thing, with which. neither law, juftice, government, nor nation hath any thing to do ; and which, unlefs in cafes of bankruptcy, is facred to the meaneft individual. As if, from the Company's books of accounts, it was poffible to difcover the caufe of abufe in the government of thofe Indian dominions : or, as if fchemes of faving to the Company, one fhilling *per* ton, freight of her cargoes : or, three pence *per* pound, in warehoufe room, would retrieve the, almoft ruined, Intereft of Britain in India.

F I N I S.

www.ingramcontent.com/pod-product-compliance
Lightning Source LLC
Chambersburg PA
CBHW030845270326
41928CB00007B/1229